December 11, 1990

John –

Your ideas, commitment,
and moral vigor have
influenced my thinking +
passions enormously.

Thank you again.

Here's to building states
+ politics that strengthen
local communities ...
and color-filled variety.

With affection,

Bruce

Growing-Up Modern

Critical Social Thought

Series editor: Michael W. Apple
Professor of Curriculum and Instruction and Educational Policy
Studies. University of Wisconsin-Madison

Already published

Growing-Up Modern

The Western State Builds Third-World Schools

BRUCE FULLER

Routledge

New York   London

Published in 1991 by

Routledge
An imprint of Routledge, Chapman and Hall, Inc.
29 West 35 Street
New York, NY 10001

Published in Great Britain by

Routledge
11 New Fetter Lane
London EC4P 4EE

Library of Congress Cataloging in Publication Data

Fuller, Bruce.
    Growing up modern: the Western state builds Third World schools/ Bruce Fuller.
       p. cm.—(Critical social thought)
    Includes bibliographical references (p.).
    ISBN 0-415-90227-4   ISBN 0-415-90228-2 (pbk.)
    1. Education and state—Africa, Southern. 2. Public schools— —Africa, Southern. 3. Teachers—Africa, Southern. I. Title. II. Series.
LC118.A356F85 1990
379.68—dc20   90-34232

British Library Cataloguing in Publication Data also available.

To Dylan who, with always fresh enthusiasm, nudges his teachers to see and encourage curiousity, challenge, and joy. And to Susan and Alta who, in very different ways, demonstrate the harmony among inquiry, affection, and the building of stronger communities.

Contents

Series Editor's Introduction

In the United States, Britain, and many other Western nations the educational system is under severe attack. It is being blamed for the decline of productivity, the loss of discipline, the destruction of standards and values, for high rates of unemployment, and so on. The list could be expanded to cover this entire page. One of the proposed, and often implemented, solutions has been to tighten control, to centralize decision-making over curricula, teaching, and evaluation. Creating more "efficient and effective" schools seemingly will provide answers to the crises in the economy and in authority relations besetting so many Western countries.[1]

Even though such proposed "solutions" may be largely misplaced, and could lead to even greater problems, the positions do signify a deep-seated faith in the power of the school. With all of the public castigation of educational means and ends, the very reason the educational system is so directly focused upon points out the power of the school in entering into the ways we commonsensically think about how to defend or alter a society's fundamental forms of life.

Such faith in the role of the school is not limited to these Western nations, however. It has been exported, along with its rationalizing and "modern" tendencies and techniques, throughout the world. In Africa, Asia, and Latin America, governments turn to the Western school to develop paths of opportunity and to enable their children to "grow up modern."

In what is called the "Third World," however, mass schooling is not delivering on its promises. In fact, this may understate the problem dramatically. Some would claim that it would not be an exaggeration to say that the modernizing project sponsored by many governments in the Third World has often simply been a failure. How are we to understand this? Why would states continue policies that are not successful and perhaps cannot succeed in the future? What are the root causes and effects of importing such Western models? In essence, the basic question may center on how we are to understand what state-sponsored formal education itself does in varied material and ideological situations.

The issue of what schools do has a long and contested history, of course. In one of the most controversial and important discussions of the social role of education, Samuel Bowles and Herbert Gintis argued that our formal institutions of schooling were not the great engines of democracy we had been led to believe. Rather, they were instruments of social control and class domination.[2] Schools sorted and selected based on students' class backgrounds. They taught different norms and values to different classes through a hidden curriculum, thereby ensuring both that the social division of labor was reproduced and that students would accept their respective rung on the occupational ladder. For all its faults, there were very real gains in this account, not least of which was that it forced us to take much more seriously the ways schools operated in a most unequal set of power relations.[3]

Behind this "correspondence theory" was a particular set of concepts, however. Schooling was directly related to the economy. "Superstructure" (anything not in the economy) was controlled by the "base" (the economy). Culture it seemed was epiphenomenal. Politics and government were also epiphenomenal. The state was organized so that it merely reproduced the needs of capital. All elements of the society worked together to guarantee the reproduction of dominance.

It soon became clear that such a theory was untenable at the level of both theory and everyday life. Its conceptual, historical, and empirical weaknesses led to a greater emphasis on what came to be called the relative autonomy of culture and politics from the economy. Immense progress was made in our understanding of the ways the economic, political, and cultural spheres of a social formation interacted and on how not only class, but gender and racial dynamics operated as sources of power.[4] In the course of this movement, our interpretations of education have become much more subtle.

The shift away from the overly economistic and reductive tendencies of the past has had a salutary effect on our understanding of the state in particular. Freed from a set of assumptions that saw all state action as totally controlled by the "needs of capital," the relationship between the state and other sectors of society and among various parts of the state itself has been especially fertile ground.[5] As Roger Dale has noted, it has also enabled us to ask a question that has too long been submerged: What difference does it make that schooling is controlled, organized, and offered by the state?[6] Thus, the connections between schooling and the state have now been opened up to serious analysis from a number of theoretical perspectives.

However, much of the more well-known work on the state and education has directed its attention to the industrialized nations of the West. This has led to decided limits on the power of our theories to explain the range of relations between schooling and the state that actually exist in the real world. It has also continued an unfortunate pattern in which too many scholars ignore the experiences of a majority of the world's population. Finally, and perhaps most importantly, policies are suggested, or simply imposed, that simply do not work. All of this increases the significance of *Growing Up Modern*.

Bruce Fuller's specific focus is on schooling and the state in the Third World. He directs our attention to three questions: What motivates state actors to expand *and* deepen the effects of mass schooling? What fiscal, administrative, and symbolic methods does the state employ, and within what constraints and contradictions, as it pursues this two-pronged agenda? What effects on teachers and children are observed (intended and unintended) as the state recurrently intervenes into the local school? In answering these questions, he criticizes, expands, and reconstructs what might be called a *signalling theory* of schooling.

To create and defend its own legitimacy, the state has used Western symbols to demonstrate that progress toward a "more modern society" is being made. However, these signals create their own problems. "As the state looks more modern, it cues high expectations that mass opportunity and choice will be broadened." These expectations are nearly impossible to meet.

These arguments show Fuller's reliance on what is known as institutional theory. Institutional theories examine the ideological role of the state. The state and the school "are viewed as parallel, often independent hosts of Western cultural commitments." They cross economic and political boundaries and "are deeply institutionalized within the worldwide network of Western polities." While such theories are not always as cognizant of how class dynamics operate nationally and internationally, there is no doubt that they require that we focus much more directly on the state itself as an institution than in many other social theories.[7] And, while *Growing Up Modern* draws a good deal of its driving force from the institutional school's emphasis on how the state and school provide basic institutional signals of what a "modern polity" should look like, Fuller is also critical of some of its assumptions and its empirical support.

This is an important point since not only is *Growing Up Modern* a truly provocative and insightful account of the dilemmas facing so many governments throughout the world, it is also a response to the many existing theories of the role of the state that stand behind the policies that states create.

Fuller argues that functional/modernist, class imposition, or institutional models not only create lifeless ideal types, but they ignore the contradictions involved in the attempts to create mass schooling. They cannot fully understand the methods state actors use in a situation where they must gain legitimacy by promising things that—given limits on existing resources and power—they cannot deliver.

Drawing on the work of Claus Offe, John Meyer, Martin Carnoy, and others, Fuller traces out the contradictory interests embodied within state policies and state action. Fuller develops a theory of the *fragile state*. Mass schooling is used to mobilize ideological commitments in favor of the central state. This mobilization depends on state elites looking like a modern state. This requires, for a variety of reasons, the expansion of mass education.

The effects of the fragile state's expansion of mass education are not what one would necessarily expect. In many nations, educational quality erodes because of the scarcity of material resources and technical expertise. Greater dependency and higher levels of debt and an increasing dependence on Western resources and institutional forms are among the results. While mass opportunity is signaled, any schooling above the primary level by and large remains extremely selective and actual wage labor growth is very slow. Affluent families reap most of the educational benefits. The fiscal crisis of the state continuously erodes the status, pay, and day to day working conditions of teachers. Bureaucratization is reinforced; centralizing tendencies that standardize school management and the curriculum and teaching in schools are increased. More modern management and pedagogical practices are proposed and signal once again that the state is truly concerned with educational quality and expanding opportunity through mass schooling. And the cycle continues.

In one of his most provocative claims, Fuller argues that "The school is used as a stage upon which political elites enact ideologies and symbols which they hold as sacred—and which enhance the process of nation building and reinforcing modern ways of growing up." Even though in many cases the state is expressly attempting to reduce class advantages and expand educational opportunity, even though the fragile state may have an interest in partly transforming society, "at the same time, core class interests must be reinforced or recast in ways that do not undercut the legitimacy, cultural ideals, or the material advantages held by economic and political elites."

In his words,

Since Third World states entered the network of Western polities quite late, highly centralized agencies must be employed to catch up, to hurry up development. Eager states attempt to quickly nationalize economic production, distribute basic commodities, deliver health services and socialize children in school. Strict regulation by the central state, of course, exacerbates the foreign and intrusive appearance of political elites as seen through local villagers' eyes. Against this backdrop, the village school is a relatively unobtrusive and inexpensive device for advancing the state's conception of socialization and mass opportunity . . . The school often fails to provide children with even basic literacy, offering no real chance for achieving higher status. But the state, collaborating with local elites, *signals* the provision of opportunity and equity. In turn, this process enhances the legitimacy and authority of traditional local leaders who now align themselves with the central state.

In this way, the state attempts to reproduce itself by using mass schooling to accumulate social capital and authority.

The operative concept here is the notion of contradiction. Educational policies and practices that attempt to create a modern school have negative effects that are brought along with them. They are positive and negative at one and the same time. They create dilemmas that may not be easily solvable under the terms of the fragile state.

One of the major strengths of *Growing Up Modern* is that while its analysis of the contradictory imperatives of the fragile state is very insightful, it does not remain only at the level of theory and policy. Rather, it takes us to the level of teachers, curricula, and students inside schools. It demonstrates the complexity of teachers' responses to the state's agenda and shows how the results are themselves the outcomes of teachers' struggles within the material circumstances in which they find themselves. This provides a good deal of support for an argument I made in *Teachers and Texts* and *Education and Power* that while *neither* teachers nor students are passive recipients of official policy and knowledge, the material and ideological conditions of daily life may produce conditions that support some elements of standardization and bureaucratization. At the same time, however, the state's overt interests may be undercut by teachers' actions on a local level. This is never cut and dried. It is always the result of compromises, daily struggles to survive in a situation that is becoming increasingly difficult.[8]

While this is a rather pessimistic (perhaps simply honest is a more appropriate word) reading of the situation, Fuller sees hope in the fact that several First and Third World states are engaging in inventive attempts to shift authority to local schools and communities. They are focusing on demonstrating effective teaching and curricular practices—often built at the local level—and are trying to broaden the craft of teaching. There are other politically and pedagogically interesting models as well that we could point to.[9] However, the point to be made is that the contradictory outcomes are *not* natural. They are very much socially produced. This means that they can be changed. We can and must alter the economic, political, and ideological relations that create the conditions so well analyzed in *Growing Up Modern*. Not to do so is to condemn so many teachers and students to lives that are not only not "modern," but may not be lives at all.

Growing Up Modern is a book that challenges many of our accepted theories of the state. This alone makes it worthwhile. But it does considerably more. It is also a book that will be critical for all those concerned with educational policy, practice and research to read and ponder. It is one of those rare volumes that challenge our accepted notions at the level of both theory and practice.

Michael W. Apple
The University of Wisconsin, Madison

Preface

Over the past century—as the Western state has coalesced and burrowed into society—faith in formal schooling also has settled into our civic psyche. In the First World, we can't get enough of it. In the Third World, earnest yet fragile states eagerly try to catch up, faithfully arguing to their people that mass education is *the* effective medicine for social ills and brittle economic growth.

Throughout the world, political leaders, education bureaucrats, and a colorful array of interest groups—with vehement bursts of energy and moral certainty—recurrently push to expand schooling, to ordain more children with the status of "student," to battle over who controls the classroom's content and ethical messages, to change teachers' behavior, and to devise new strategies for deepening the school's effect on children.

Even when it seems that all possible children have been pulled into the temple of secular schooling, the bullish state and school institution define ever younger children as eligible for *pre*school or declare that all adults must be subjected to institutionalized treatments, such as *life-long learning*.

At times thoughtful political actors or local activists raise constructively critical questions about the state's relentless support of mass schooling. Can the school help retrieve local community, accommodating the values, languages, and work of pluralistic groups? Can teachers more consistently motivate children to read, to craft ideas, to pursue their own curiosities—rather than sitting passively as receptacles of homogenous "facts"? Can schooling more effectively reduce, rather than legitimate and reinforce, social class advantages ascribed to elite groups? Can the state enhance the teaching craft, rather than mechanically treating teachers as passive objects of school reform?

But the Western state is uneasy about confronting such penetrating questions. Political actors' faith in universal, bureaucratic forms of growing up is simply too strong. Mass schooling seems like such a benevolent device for advancing the modern state's *nation-wide* agenda—using education to integrate national markets, to smooth out the rough edges of cultural diversity, to build meritocratic rules for demonstrating secular achievement and for getting ahead. Certainly no sane political actor gets in the way of the state's historical desire to expand mass schooling and to deepen its effects on children.

This book explores why, and how, the Western state so vigorously engages in this dual agenda: First, building and spreading the institution of mass schooling, then intensifying efforts to boost the school's effectiveness. This term *effectiveness* is slippery but usually refers to deepening the imprint that the school attempts to leave on the child's heart and mind. We will delve into three specific questions over the course of this volume:

- What motivates state actors to expand and deepen the effects of mass schooling?
- What fiscal, administrative, and symbolic methods does the state employ, and within what constraints and contradictions, as it pursues this two-pronged agenda?
- What effects on teachers and children are observed (intended and unintended) as the state recurrently tries to intervene into the local school?

The Political Utility of Mass Schooling

This book focuses on one version of the Western state, what I call the *fragile state*. Here nationalist leaders within young polities must—to advance their own legitimacy—construct modern-looking institutions. Yet the fragile state's credibility is highly constrained, as are its fiscal and organizational resources. Third World adaptations of the Western state are plopped down within quite un-Western, pre-modern societies. The fragile state's tentative rise in Third World settings ignites strong popular expectations that secular leaders will transform society, bringing *modern progress*. To reinforce state institutions, however, political actors must form *interdependencies* with (a) pre-modern or feudal economic interests, (b) an urban middle class that demands jobs and modern forms of status, and/or (c) loose collections of rural ethnic groups which hardly form, even resist being pulled into, a cohesive polity.

The second half of this book focuses on the African state's interdependent relationship with mass schooling. The contrasts and contradictions facing African political elites are fascinating. While eager to build an integrated modern nation, African states face demands from groups and institutions that question Western political-economic ideals. These include: village chiefs that see traditional forms of authority and socialization eroding; post-colonial economic firms that would not benefit from opening up liberal markets; and an urban middle class that demands opportunity for *their* families first, and for rural groups later.

In mediating this kaleidoscopic array of interests, the institution of mass schooling holds enormous political utility. Within Africa mass schooling has become an unquestioned device for extending membership in these fledgling polities. *Growing up modern* has become the universal treatment for pulling youth and families into the nation-state. Mass schooling has become a key strategy for signaling modern institutional change, particularly the coming of Western ideals and the arrival of mass opportunity. Building more schools is like building more post offices—it symbolizes the state's growing capacity to construct modern, be they modest, organizations. Whether children actually are learning, or the mail is delivered on time, does not really worry political actors. The fragile state's primary agenda is to symbolically and visibly penetrate the rural hinterlands and urban shantytowns.

By relying on *signals* of mass opportunity and meritocratic rules of getting ahead, the state can display Western ideals without directly attacking pre-modern economic interests and social organization. Of course, once the state signals the coming of modernity, popular demand grows for prompt delivery on its political-economic promises. And fragile states lack sufficient material resources, organizational infrastructure, and technical know-how to deliver concrete improvements in economic and social well-being.

We will explore the internal action of states at two distinct organizational levels: (a) at the state's institution-level game of putting up more classrooms and related symbols of mass opportunity, and (b) at the level of technical strategies and rituals employed to boost educational quality, to deepen the school's effect on children. Some state actors, education bureaucrats, and professional educators are actually serious about raising how much children learn in the classroom. And a subset of inventive political actors are attempting to empower local schools to serve the interests of local communities, even seeking to better motivate teachers and advance their craft. We will explore how, and why, some state actors are willing to de-link the local school from the central state's traditional agenda.

More "mature" states and government organizations, such as those found in the United States or Europe, also face recurring uncertainties within their cultural and economic environs. In turn, political leaders mobilize the symbols and organizational levers within the school institution to attack these exigencies—whether the polity's ills are defined as economic decline, unemployment, cultural centrifugation, or the (perennial) moral decay of our youth. This book focuses largely on The Third World which provides sharp images of the state's interdependence and use of mass schooling to *transform traditional society*. Yet this discussion will reveal how, in the First World, increasingly brittle states are acting to *reinforce* the bureaucratic and uniform cultural elements of *modern society*. By focusing on the fragile state, and its interdependence with the school institution, we will learn more about why and how established states (often sailing on uncertain seas) attempt to cajole or control teachers and schools.

My enthusiasm for writing this book springs from two observations that both intrigue and deeply trouble me. First, Third World governments are under enormous pressure to deliver mass opportunity and "modern progress." The rapid expansion of education and its bureaucratized form of control does signal to local peoples that modern change is on the way. But the wait for modernity's arrival is getting longer and longer in much of the developing world. Mass schooling, despite rapid expansion and attempts at centralized control, is *not* delivering on its promises.

In the First World, both the political Left and Right are disappointed that mass schooling is failing to deliver on its claimed economic and social effects. So, a wide spectrum of political actors and educators are turning to classic bureaucratic patterns of reform. These include: tightening controls over, and routinizing, how teachers work; homogenizing curricula into easily testable bits and pieces; and legitimating unquestionable "facts" and technical knowledge as *the* optimal form of knowledge and human inquiry. Struggling to look more modern, Third World states and educators are adopting these centralized administrative remedies. These strategies for tightening up on schools are not new in Africa where colonial forms of administration still define "modern management."

How has the Western state—originally dedicated to respect for plural communities and democratic forms of economy—arrived at this widespread faith in such a bureaucratic form of socialization for our children? Why does the Western state's rhetoric about individual development and democratic forms of learning so deeply contradict the corporate form of institutional control impressed upon the local school, and forced upon the objectified teacher?

Second, I am perplexed by the simplistic ways in which both intellectuals and "policymakers" view the motivations, actions, and effects of the state. We tend to see political actors either as pursuing "the common good" or as reinforcing their own interests (and those of their fellow economic elites). Recent scholarship has sharpened a more careful understanding of the state's behavior, and that of the school institution, as they weave their way through society, often out of the reach and control of elite groups. I emphasize that both the state and the school do possess clear boundaries and coherent interests, but each must form interdependencies with other institutions (both local and central organizations). Simply to build and reinforce their own institutional legitimacy, both state and school must display Western symbols and advance modern expectations and promises. I focus on the contradictions which stem from this paradox between building an organizational identity versus forming required interdependencies for gaining material resources and social legitimacy.

This book sprouted from my work in the Third World over the past decade, first as a graduate student, then as a staff member within two international agencies. My curiosity in comparing First and Third World states originated during a recent stint within the U.S. Department of State (*USAID*)—where understandings of the Third World are heavily colored by the American state's own ideological and economic interests.

My longer time at the World Bank revealed how little we know about the internal workings of the Western state, as it omnipotently acts upon, and digs under the skin of, Third World societies. After the Great Society, the Reagan Revolution, and parallel movements in the Third World, none of my colleagues in Washington see the central state or idealized free markets as *the* panacea for national development. When we drift to the middle ground between state and market, we feel suddenly exposed, ignorant of how political institutions operate and how they attempt to improve, to boost economic vitality, and to raise the quality of life within pluralistic societies. Here Western governments, scholars, and their theories are severely underdeveloped. Compared to the West, Third World states are accumulating much more experience in improving public organizations' capacity to spark economic innovation *and* to more gently respect and advance cultural variety.

Several mentors and colleagues have taught me much about statecraft and the multifaceted importance of schooling within the logic of Western politics and ideology. John Vasconcellos and Craig Fuller have been with me for some time, providing colorfully diverse ideas, debate, and reality tests. The way I see the state and school also has been heavily influenced by the work of Martin Carnoy, Sandy Dornbusch, Emile Durkheim, Maurice Garnier, Jerry Hage, John W. Meyer, Claus Offe, Chiqui Ramirez, and Ricky Rubinson.

Colleagues in Washington have raised a rainbow of competing ideas about what national development actually means, for both elites and local peoples. Occasionally, we even talk about how the West's development agencies can work more critically, with less presumption, as we fiddle with the institutions and mores of other societies. Looking toward Washington, I have many thanks to offer Victor Barnes, Cliff Block, Ron Bonner, Joan Claffey, Dennis de Trey, Aklilu Habte, Steve Heyneman, Anjimile Kapakasa, Emmanuel Jimenez, Marlaine Lockheed, Max Sawicky, Nwanganga Shields, Neeta Sirur, David Sprague, Gary Theisen, and Michael Ward. They have provided financial and moral support for my work in Africa. They have spurred me to think more carefully about why development projects succeed and often fail.

Michael Apple has given essential encouragement and constructive criticism at key points over the life of this project. He has pushed me to clarify my definition of, and description of processes within, the state. Michael's own writings have helped me see more sharply the interaction between state and school. The editorial staff at Routledge press have been very thorough and gracious. Harvard University has provided a warm and invigorating setting within which I completed this book.

My friends and colleagues in Botswana, Ethiopia, and Malawi provided the real grist for this book. I wish that mention of each by name was possible without risk of jeopardizing their own positions. They have constantly moved me to reflect and write—as I listen to their observations, critiques, dilemmas, and especially their dreams of how institutions might operate more efficaciously *and* with more respect for diverse communities. Wes Snyder has been an engaging, essential intellectual partner in southern Africa. My African colleagues most certainly will disagree with facets of how I see their states and schools. Any errors in description or interpretation are mine. Names of schools and individuals used in the book are fictitious but represent real actors and observed events.

Most of all my thanks go to Susan Holloway who constantly insists on realism in my ideas and clarity in my explanations. She rightfully nudges me to balance the numbers, the analysis, the theory with a personal commitment to strengthen and enjoy our immediate community. Otherwise, we miss the ultimate human aims of our intellectual musings.

Finally, thanks to Paul Goodman for writing *Growing-up Absurd*. Thank you all.

Bruce Fuller
Cambridge, Massachusetts

Speaking of the family, let's turn to a matter on the mind of every American tonight—education. We all know the sorry story of the sixties and seventies—soaring spending, plummeting test scores—and that hopeful trend of the eighties when we replaced an obsession with dollars with a commitment to quality, and test scores started back up. There is a lesson here that we should all write on the blackboard a hundred times—in a child's education, money can never take the place of basics like discipline, hard work, and, yes, homework.

—Ronald Reagan (1988)

Nairobi, Kenya—President Daniel arap Moi yesterday called on Christians in Africa to hold on more tenaciously to the principles of their faith in order to rid the continent of the twin evils of tribalism and division. He called on Christians to pay special attention to the conditions of the youth, particularly teenagers in school so that they were not lead (sic) astray. The President told those responsible for running schools to ensure that errant teachers were not overly protected at the expense of children in their classes.

—Sunday Kenyan Times (1988)

I accuse the Ministry of Education because it is failing to reach the needs of the young generation, whom we now call students, rather than the leaders of tomorrow. The Ministry distorts their future because it is failing to provide jobs for them. Recent strikes by teachers, were only a dress rehearsal for things to come. The Ministry should build more junior secondary schools to give failers an opportunity to repeat. Our parents are worried because after 12 years of expenditures they expect something from us. To ignore the masses' grievances is a suicidal (sic) and inconsiderate.

—Letter from a secondary school graduate
to the Botswana Guardian (1988)

It is, then, up to the State to remind the teacher constantly of the ideas, the sentiments that must be impressed upon the child to adjust him to the milieu in which he must live.

Religious beliefs are the *representations* which express the nature of sacred things and the relations which they sustain, either with each other or with profane things. . . . Rituals are the rules of conduct which prescribe how men should behave in relation to sacred things . . . [and these] sacred things are simply collective ideals that have fixed themselves on material objects.

—Emile Durkheim (1925)

1

A Faithful Yet Rocky Romance
Between State and School

Unannounced, I was rushed into a haphazardly built shelter, a stark room bounded by crumbling brick walls and window frames absent their glass panes. That stale odor—found in any small humid space filled with active sweating bodies—hit me first. Then the rustling of bare feet against a dusty concrete floor could be heard as eighty-five small children, most dressed in fading blue uniforms, sprang to their feet. A seemingly automatic welcome came forth loud and clear, "Good morning, sir!" I recollected with self-conscious discomfort a British novel where the colonial administrator is loudly greeted by his subjects.

This was my premiere visit to an African classroom. I have observed kids in Mexican schools. I grew up in North American classrooms. Never before had I witnessed so many children packed into such a barren classroom. Nor had I felt this disciplined self-subordination so deeply ingrained in children so young.

The State's Faith in Mass Schooling

As I spend more time sitting in African classrooms, I have come to see that such obligatory salutes are mixed with warm informality, lively spontaneity, and indifferent passivity among pupils and teachers alike. Classrooms also become less crowded by grade 5 or 6, as youths drop out to work the family's land, or to work the streets selling gum or shining shoes. But that first impression—seeing those youngsters' deep faith in Western schooling and their reflexive loyalty to impersonal authority—crisply captured how the modern state requires children to grow up. These sharp images from African classrooms accent the two basic questions explored in this book.

The first question is: *What forces have historically pushed the relentless spread of Western schooling worldwide?* Since the sixteenth-century Reformation, political leaders and commercial elites, in capitals and villages alike, have preached the virtues of formal schooling. The liberal state of the nineteenth century, emerging from revolutions in North America and France, intensified the fight over who should control how children grow up.[1] Since World War II, civic elites have convinced parents that being "modern" requires sending your child to the secular school.[2] Getting ahead requires more school credentials, even "life-long learning" in formal institutions. *Pre*schools and child care must be expanded to serve young children and infants as parents intensify their own individual pursuit of economic security, status, and personal expression.

The Western state, for two centuries now, has turned reflexively to the school to address a variety of social maladies. No other institution within the secular civic sphere has gained the intense faith now held in mass schooling. The medicinal magic of schooling is applied to a variety of public troubles—whether "the national problem" is defined as lack of economic competitiveness, lack of moral character, incorporating minority groups into the mainstream, or getting kids away from drugs or into more rational sex.[3]

Fragile States, Frustrations of Faith

The state—simply one bounded institution—is not the sole force pushing the explosive growth of mass schooling. The Western polity's now sacred commitment to socializing our children in modern bureaucratic schools stems from historical demands of several institutions: churches that hoped to boost literacy and comprehension of the Bible; modest shop owners and traders who still link schooling to modern skills and status; larger firms and industrialists who prefer literate workers; and parents who have come to associate formal schooling and literacy with economic opportunity. We will look at the state's efficacy within this context of competing institutions, each advancing particularistic ideals and material agendas.

This book does focus on the Western state, especially how its motivations, methods, and influence come to life within Third World societies. I am most curious about how political actors in *fragile states*, or aging states sailing on turbulent seas, reach out to the school institution to advance their own legitimacy. Unsteady states, pushing the liberal bundle of symbols inherent within mass schooling, often confront sharp counter forces: parents who demand their children's labor at home, in the fields, or in the streets to help eke out a cash income; village leaders who resist government schools and the associated subversion of traditional authority; conservative elites who hope to contain expectations of mass opportunity; churches that seek to retain their control over the socialization of children; and small-scale employers who demand the low-cost labor of children and youth.

The fragile state can ill-afford to ignore these resisting groups. Overly aggressive pursuit of liberal ideals, expressed in part through mass schooling, often alienates conservative forces and shatters the already brittle state. But in order to look modern and to signal mass opportunity the Third World state must express faith in, and materially expand, schooling. Thus, most fragile states pursue a rather rocky romance with the school. My view of the state—particularly its fragility within uncertain institutional environments and its expressive use of the school—also pertains to more mature states within Europe or North America. Illustrative similarities with more stable states will be drawn.

Contradictions Facing the State

Third World states face the deep popular expectation that mass schooling connotes the spread of mass opportunity. Indeed, since World War II newly independent nations have invested enormous resources in secular schooling. The capacity of post-colonial governments to put up schools has been phenomenal. The proportion of children attending primary school in developing countries has doubled in the past three decades, rising from 35 percent in 1950, to 75 percent in 1990. Today 120 million more children are enrolled in primary school than were attending just a decade ago (now totaling 500 million). In Africa, the number of children attending school continues to grow at 5 percent a year, far surpassing population growth and despite only slight economic growth.[4]

Brittle Third World states, already overtaxed and suffering from shaky political and economic foundations, have invested heavily in Western-style schools. Rapid construction of more schools, as detailed below, serves a variety of state interests: reducing barriers among tribes that speak different languages, encouraging economic integration and

3

entry to the wage economy, building individual loyalty to the nation-state rather than to tribal or religious authority, and (allegedly) boosting economic productivity and growth.

Most Third World states have sparked enormous popular demand for schooling, as political elites earnestly try to signal modern institutions and forms of opportunity. But the state's resources have not kept pace with growth in child populations and enrollment rates. As economic growth has levelled-off or dissolved, eroding government resources are being spread over more and more students. Already minimal levels of educational quality are declining even further. In many countries rapid post-colonial expansion of the civil service and the wage sector is proving unsustainable. Teacher paychecks appear months late; rising foreign debt brings government cutbacks; private capital dries up; streets, civic buildings, and brick classrooms are literally crumbling. As parents see the wage sector collapsing and fail to see teachers showing up at school (until they are paid), absolute enrollments are falling, for the first time, in several countries. Already fragile states must redouble their struggle to maintain quality and deepen the effects of mass schooling, even revert to rekindling popular demand for mass schooling.[5]

Despite the severity and urgency of these issues, policy-makers and local activists know little about the state's discrete influence in quickening (or slowing) the rate of school expansion. Enormous expectations are held for the modern state's capacity to expand schooling and provide minimal levels of literacy. Frustrations over the state's actual efficacy are equally great. This book argues that we must think more carefully about the antecedents that push the state's faithful romance with the school, and about the forms of state action that are more (or less) effective in expanding and improving mass schooling. Empirical evidence is accumulating on the state's influence, much of which I will review.

Deepening the Faith

Beyond the imperative to expand mass education, the Western state (whether fragile or stable) also struggles *to deepen the school's effect on children*. In the Third World, the contemporary issue is defined as "declining educational quality." Similarly, in Europe and North America the recurring issue has been the balance between expanding access to schooling (for all ethnic groups and social classes) versus advancing

4

educational quality. Contemporary political leaders and educators in the United States speak of raising "school effectiveness."[6]

I frame the state's involvement with school improvement in a more explicit way by asking: *How efficacious is the state in creating, then reinforcing, bureaucratic rules and a rationalized moral order within the classroom?* This is the second major issue addressed in this book. The question speaks to whether, and under what conditions, centralized political elites can *deepen the effects of schooling*, reshaping the consciousness and social rules that children come to abide by.[7] The bureaucratic tightening of what is taught, and how, is not necessarily the only way by which the central state might attempt to improve educational quality or pupil achievement. It is, however, the most common strategy—whether we look at recurrent "progressive" school reform in the United States or post-colonial schools in the Third World.[8]

The dramatic construction of more and more schools demonstrates the modern state's ample legitimacy in displacing traditional means of child socialization. This event does *not* necessarily mean that the state is effective in transforming the teacher's daily practices or the classroom's social rules. Prior theorists claim that their models validly explain the forces which drive the expansion *and* deepening of the Western school, failing to see that antecedent processes and actual effects may be quite different for each outcome. The state has long tried to implement hierarchical forms of authority and social rules within the school, first mimicking the structure of fifteenth-century Catholic administration, then drawing from the magic and legitimacy of nineteenth-century industrial factories.[9] But has this mimickry of "modern administration" actually influenced the behavior and motivation of teachers, or the performance of students? We will look inside Third World schools and classrooms to see how (and when) the state actually touches the rules and moral order which pattern how children grow up.

Why does the Western state, and political actors within, so vehemently push to expand, and alter the quality of, schooling? *How* do government activists exercise their ideals, resources, and regulatory controls? And what *actual effects* result from this tireless action by the state? These are the central questions that we will explore throughout this book.

Energizing the State's Pursuit of Sacred Rules and Sacred Knowledge

I argue that the state, quite often, is *not* effective in deepening the school's effects. This recurring frustration then spurs the state to redouble

5

efforts aimed at shaping the behavior of teachers and children. In plural polities the school faces great difficulty in socializing low-status minorities (or non-modern tribes) to accept mainstream behaviors and rules of achievement. Black American youths, for instance, often remain loyal to the rules of membership reproduced in their own peer or ethnic circles. Concern in the United States over recurring declines in test scores, despite expanding school expenditures, is another example of the state's limited capacity to actually deepen the school's effects. This can threaten the state or particular governments, for Western-looking political elites must display competence in harmonizing plural beliefs and behavior into a common moral order.

Overall, the school's capacity to impress a common moral order is quite impressive. Anthropologist Robert Everhart, for instance, recently examined the meanings that children associate with the words "work" and "play" when they are at school. He found that children define "work" as activities guided and enforced by the teacher, whereas classroom tasks initiated or elaborated by the student were viewed as enjoyable "play." This is a powerful instance in which the school unobtrusively assigns certain meaning to an authority relationship (between teacher and pupil) and to individual action. This particular meaning of "work" is not questioned; in fact it is legitimated and institutionalized by the school. This is a moral lesson, what Emile Durkheim would call a "sacred (undoubted) social fact." No particular bit of knowledge is being taught explicitly. Mass schooling quietly communicates to the child a moral order and classification scheme, the understanding of which is critical if the child is to grasp the meaning of "work" in adult organizations.[10]

In the Third World, a major educational issue is whether schools have any lasting impact on the literacy, behavior, and beliefs of youth. As schools pop up in rural villages and urban shanty towns, the state signals modernity and opportunity. But the school's actual effects—boosting literacy, encouraging innovative farming practices, changing health or sexual practices—often are disappointing. In much of the Third World, half of all children do not even complete primary school, greatly limiting intended social and economic effects. Traditional forms of socialization and immediate labor demands placed on children, as well as conventional roles and behavior, swamp the state's earnest attempt to have children grow up modern.

The state's recurring impotence prompts political and educational leaders to redouble their efforts aimed at expanding the school's presence and deepening its impact on children. Ever since the modern state successfully wrestled child socialization into the civic sphere, political leaders have worried about educational quality. Technical remedies are commonly mounted by the state: pupil exams are standardized and given with greater frequency; teachers are evaluated more tightly; the curriculum is simplified to focus on easily-tested bits of knowledge.

Yet administrative remedies often run aground, due to their high cost or inability to touch the uncertain technical process of teaching and learning. Political elites, frustrated by the limited capacity of the state apparatus to control teachers' local behavior, engage in symbolic action to at least encourage certain moral commitments and behavioral choices. So we see presidents of the United States talking about the need for more homework, as a signal that children must work harder. We see elites of all political colors arguing that teachers must demand higher student performance if the nation is to become more competitive economically. And we see Third World education ministers encouraging more instruction in math and computing, symbolizing how schooling must look more modern. Throughout the book we will explore the state's means for attempting influence, including budgetary, administrative, and symbolic action.

Organization of the Book

Remaining portions of this chapter describe why, and how, the state vigorously pursues these parallel agendas: expanding *and* deepening mass schooling. These twin agendas present contradictions and complementarities for fragile, resource-poor states. In turn, contradictions and constraints push political elites to build interdependencies—with Western ideals and deep expectations of the state, with economic organizations, and with the local school institution. This leads me to a novel conception of the fragile state, one which departs from earlier functionalist and deterministic portrayals (based on European and North American images of the state). I will sketch my model of the state in the present chapter and will illuminate this model more fully in subsequent chapters.

Chapter 2 reviews earlier theories of state and school. This review focuses on the basic facets of state action: its motivations, strategies for attempting influence or control, and actual effects within schools. I emphasize that models used to explain the *expansion* of schooling are not always relevant in understanding the state's efforts to *deepen* the institution's effects.

Chapter 3 then presents life within one fragile state, Malawi, located in southern Africa. I focus on the abundant contradictions stemming from African political elites' struggle to construct a Western-like state apparatus and ideology in the face of limited fiscal capacity and constrained civic authority.

In Chapter 4 we move inside the Third World school, asking whether and, if so, *how* the state actually touches the actions and beliefs of teachers and students. The state may rapidly expand schooling, yet hold little influence in shaping the classroom's social rules and the teacher's normative actions. The state in Africa, on the other hand, exercises a rich ideological and symbolic agenda, manifest in uniform curricula and routinized teaching practices. Third World states, learning from their colonial administrators, often attempt to manage schooling through strict, centralized regimes. This chapter stems from my ongoing work inside southern African classrooms.

Chapter 5 concludes the volume by asking, How can the fragile state better serve pluralistic communities while reinforcing its own institutional integrity? Two basic forces will persistently operate, perhaps intensify, within the Third World. Political elites will push, with tireless resolve, to strengthen central state institutions. This will require strong interdependencies with economic elites and other groups committed to nation-building, including groups interested in Western-style rationalization of economic activity, social organization, and even local rules. But this push toward universal, impersonal forms of social organization will be countered by a second resilient force: the expression and reinforcement of local, ethnic communities. How the brittle state might better mediate these conflicting, often fatal pressures is the subject of the concluding chapter. Examples of how more secure and gentle states might reinforce local community are discussed.

Fragile Versions of the Western State

The *fragile state* bobs up and down in an ocean filled with uncertainties and hazards. Occasionally, the state's buoyancy fails and certain governments, agencies, or actors vanish beneath the surface. We often see particular governments come and go—whether looking at Third

World or First World nations. The ideology or structure of particular state organizations also changes. But let's define two key features of the fragile state, as a method for understanding why elements of the state do change or disappear, and how political elites actively attempt to resist (or hurry) these transformations.

First, the state's fragility is manifest in its urgent need to nurture *interdependencies with other institutions* that operate in the surrounding environment. These links to other elite groups and local communities are essential to the fragile state—an institution that perennially suffers from scarcities of social legitimacy, material resources, and technical know-how.

These interdependencies flow *upward* in the sense that a particular Third World state draws down or borrows the expectations, secular authority, liberal ideals, and bureaucratic forms that are sacred and accepted within the Western state.

These interdependencies also operate *laterally* in terms of linking economic elites with firms, churches, and labor unions. And these interdependencies can be seen as moving *downward* in that the central state often attempts to build and control subordinate institutions. I will argue that the institution of mass schooling can operate in either a lateral or a subordinate fashion vis-a-vis political elites, depending on their relative historical strength. Very often the fragile state draws legitimacy from the (earlier established) school institution, using it as a stage upon which the ideals and symbols of the liberal polity are enacted.

The second essential characteristic of the fragile state is that as it attempts to manage these interdependencies, a second round of *uncertainty, contradiction, and technical ambiguity* haunts the political apparatus. Contradictions inherent in constructing mass institutions that can actually deliver mass opportunity are particularly troublesome. In the name of equal or mass opportunity, for example, the secular state has historically moved to incorporate diverse church or municipal schools into a standardized "system." Following national independence, and anxious to lessen constraints of race, class, and caste, centralized Third World states promptly took over colonial school systems and pushed standardization of curricula, teacher preparation, and school management.

"Government schools" are then portrayed as boosting powerful Western ideals: unifying disparate tribes into an integrated market and cultural frame; replacing ascriptive, particularistic forms of merit and status (reinforced by village and religious authorities) with achieved, universal

9

forms (enforced by central secular authorities); and directly linking the reified individual to the state (via "citizenship" and civic "rights"), setting aside the mediating authority of local collectives. But the pursuit of liberal ideals, usually under a corporate state apparatus, can alienate traditional forms of authority—be it the village headman, nationwide churches, or elites who control consolidated capital. Leaders of fragile states must artfully manage this first contradiction.[11]

Another contradiction should be emphasized: Popular association of *mass schooling* with *mass opportunity* will be credible only if the state displays a sustained capacity to expand education and to ensure minimal levels of quality. Explosive expansion of schooling in immediate post-colonial eras is critical in signaling the opening of opportunity under Western meritocratic terms. Yet many governments have overextended their limited fiscal resources and technical human capacities. Static government budgets, rising foreign debt, and relentless population growth in contemporary times have undercut educational quality. As the school's effectiveness deteriorates, and employment in the wage sector levels off, elites and local villagers alike come to realize that mass schooling is simply a symbolic device holding little utility in actually providing new opportunity. This slowly subverts the state's legitimacy.

This book details action emanating from within the state—motivations of political actors, strategies for exerting influence, and actual effects in shaping behavior within schools and classrooms. In sum, these two *conditions*—the level of contradiction and competition within the institutional environment *and* the state's own capacity to manage interdependencies to reduce uncertainty—bound the fragile state's range of credible action and its likely efficacy.

Toward A Textured View of the State

I have trouble reading through current theories of the state. Existing models—whether they emphasize liberal-democratic, class-imposition, relative autonomy, or institutional features of political organization—tend to present lifeless ideal-types. This fails to capture the methods enacted by political actors, and the hazards through which they must move in attempting to gain popular legitimacy and resources, and in exerting influence over others. The dynamic character of the state over time often is lost: its environment, its own credibility and technical capacity, and the level of individual agency within state organizations.

When reading such deterministic representations of the state, I often recall a short story concerning two brothers in the early 1980s. The first, working as domestic affairs advisor to President Ronald Reagan, could feel the political opportunity close at hand. Mr. Reagan's secretary of education was about to release a report on schooling, emphasizing that quality and "excellence" must be addressed. Failure to act would further undercut America's economic competitiveness and worsen the alleged decay of young Americans' moral fiber. This savvy advisor was eager to construct a centrist position for Mr. Reagan on any domestic issue. The economy was in deep recession. Criticism was intensifying that the president simply ignored the country's social ills. Arrangements were made quickly to have Mr. Reagan preside over the report's public release. During the subsequent year, the president's speeches increasingly addressed educational quality, spurring what became a decade-long nationwide movement for "educational excellence."

The second brother, at this time, was helping to devise a new education initiative for California's liberal governor. In the coming year, this politician would run for the United States Senate; thus he was anxious to stake out a centrist position on an issue that could draw broad support. Crafted through speeches, press releases, and legislation, *the* issue pushed by the ambitious governor was that of raising the quality and clout of public schooling.

Both brothers deeply believed that the state and their very different administrations should become active in the education arena. Mobilizing symbols commonly linked to better schools—economic progress, human investment, and moral determination—also aided their bosses. In the end, this constructed interdependency between the state and the school sparked infusions of material capital to education *and* political capital to the state-crafters.

To date, general sketches of the state hold limited utility for those of us who have battled within, or against, government. First, this tale illustrates how actors within the state attempt to read and manage uncertain environments. Some students of the state, from traditional functionalist or "strong state" viewpoints, often assume that political institutions act with autonomy and material effectiveness. Competing theorists, working from Marxist or European structuralist perspectives, argue that the state is passively embedded in the interests of economic and cultural elites. Neither view captures the frequency and ways in which state actors hustle to manage interdependencies within their environment, then use these ideological and institutional allies to mobilize resources and technical methods within the state apparatus.[12]

Second, the story shows how theories of the state fail to differentiate between two levels of action. Politicians' press releases, speeches, or appearances at schools aim to *build* or reinforce two institutions—mass schooling *and* the state. This higher level of institution-building does serve to sanction the lower-level, more technical task of *deepening* the school's effects. But the state's motivations, strategies, and actual influence with regard to deepening schooling often are different. Broad models of the state rarely differentiate between these two levels at which institutions are built, then intensified locally.[13]

Third, the story of two brothers illustrates how individuals are occasionally effective in bumping resources and symbols toward mass schooling (and away from the military, economic interests, or other social sectors). My view of the state—looking from the inside out—struggles with the issue of individual agency. Prior theories tend to ignore the diverse and contentious character of individual actors (and their coalitions) within state organizations. In the Third World, agents of Western-style development certainly are efficacious over historical periods in changing the underlying structure of political-economy. On the other hand, deep institutional structures, including expectations of legitimate action and levers available within the Western state, constrain how the individual can move.

Defining the Fragile State Within an Uncertain Polity

Next, I explicitly sketch the fragile state's four basic features. My work with Third World governments influences how I visualize state action. I also draw on experience within less fragile political institutions, including a provincial legislature, the U.S. Department of State, and the World Bank. My portrayal of the state should be viewed as one set of tentative assertions—images to be weighed against the evidence presented in the remaining chapters.

1. The State's Position and Boundaries

Students of the state are preoccupied with defining its boundaries and its (functional) posture relative to other organizations, including organizations of economy, church, and family. Political theorists have tried to pin down the ideological and economic positioning of state organizations, often making static and universal claims about their affiliation with particular classes or groups, be they distinguished by liberal-democratic, capitalist, or bureaucratic interests. Deterministic images of the state's motivations and actions dominate these theoretical perspectives (as we will discuss in Chapter Two).

I emphasize that the fragile version of the Western state is a *bounded institution* containing (oft borrowed) internal motivations, ideals, social rules, and rituals. Balanced against a desire to reinforce its own organizational integrity, the fragile state operates in a *highly uncertain environment*. The school—as a separate bounded institution—can potentially become a tool of the state as political elites attempt to broaden and reinforce their own legitimate authority over civil society. Yet building interdependence with the school prompts numerous uncertainties, technical difficulties, and material strains on the state's resources.

I also highlight how intense popular expectations for the fragile state to deliver modernity run head-on into these environmental uncertainties and frustrations. In turn, the besieged state moves to build, then deepen the effects of, affiliated institutions (like the school). The state's ideological and material positioning within the polity and economy, of course, are important. But uncertainties stemming from the state's position—be it aggressive and strong, or reactive and weak—drive inventive action, as political elites reach out to build interdependencies with other institutions. My focus is on understanding these forms of interplay and action, not on inferring static institutional position and role.

The state's capacity to accumulate economic resources and social legitimacy depends upon its ability to advance a *mix of interests*. Actors within the fragile state, when too closely aligned with singular interests (be they landed, capitalist, worker, peasant, religious, or state-bureaucratic interests), risk serious challenge from disenfranchised groups. Here I draw heavily on the work of Claus Offe, who sees the state as an independent mediator of conflict among various social classes and groups. Offe argues that the state at times must position itself independently of economic elites, given its role as mediator.[14]

13

The fragile state sometimes gains political advantage when it *loudly* disengages from the interests of economic elites—broadening its popular support. Offe clearly acknowledges that political elites must respond to economic interests, in part, to accumulate economic capital for public projects. But the state, for its own reinforcement and reproduction, also must worry about its level of political capital and breadth of popular authority. When the credibility of political elites erodes, their capacity to tax, raise foreign capital, or manage the economy also deteriorates, undercutting the state's material foundations.[15]

The fragile state's desire to stake out a distinct position, then to reinforce and extend its organizational boundaries requires two forms of institution-building. First, political actors must construct new central agencies, including organizations which engage in taxation, rule-making, policing, and production. This requires drawing-in both material capital and social authority. To gain authority, political elites must persuasively assert that they are acting like a Western state, expressing the associated mix of liberal-democratic, capitalist, and meritocratic rules of opportunity. Such expressions (symbolically or materially) affect domestic legitimacy and increasingly determine access to Western capital and foreign aid.

Second, the state must construct a distinct institutional position, by eroding or co-opting traditional forms of community and authority. By broadening its own jurisdiction, and crafting requisite symbols of the "modern polity," the state self-confidently reinforces its authority and dominance within the non-private civic sphere.

The battle over *who* should control the socialization of children is one important example of this phenomenon. The Western state, for two centuries now, has attempted to minimize the roles of the family, church, and village leaders in how children are brought up. Mass schooling represents *the* modern form of socialization, allegedly enhancing Western ideals of rationality, meritocratic opportunity, and equality. Effective wearing down of local collectives, which lay outside the state-defined civic sphere, depends partly upon the *economic* resources of political elites. In addition, fragile states must mobilize *ideological commitments and signals* which convince parents and local elites that mass schooling is a legitimate form of socialization, providing youth access to, and higher status within, the wage economy and modern society. Alternatively, where the village school is already deeply rooted within local collectives, the state must persuade local churches, chiefs, and parents that incorporation and standardization of schooling will better serve civic ideals, including the sweet promise of mass opportunity.[16]

2. The State's Interdependence with Two Environments

Theorists have long seen the state as functionally advancing the West's social and economic ideals. Those on the political Right argue that the classically liberal state will allow markets to flourish and individual rights to blossom through democratic forms of cooperation. From the Left, the state is seen as falling far short of these ideals, instead advancing the economic advantages, social rules, and idioms held by elites.[17] Both these versions of functionalism presume a constant institutional environment, that is, the strength of surrounding organizations is seen as constant. Functionalist theory also assumes that political elites rarely build boundaries around the state which allow alternative values and social rules to grow within. Nor can the state bridge over to previously disenfranchised groups in ways that bounce back to modify the character and normative interests of the state itself.

Third World states, not unlike the United States, originally emerged in opposition to colonial orders, narrow polities dominated by foreign business and culture, as well as caste forms of opportunity. *Post*-colonial political elites must gain economic resources to build civic institutions and to reproduce the nationalist state structure. But political actors' legitimacy can be severely undercut when they align themselves too closely with commercial elites. The fragile state's recurrent practice of incorporating firms into the state structure is the clearest way of containing previously independent economic interests (or at least ensuring that political elites share in the bounty yielded by "public enterprises").

More broadly, political actors within any Western state must demonstrate that they can deliver modernity and "progress." Here the state's authority is signaled through economic growth, construction of civic institutions, and by nurturing meritocratic paths of opportunity. Political actors can draw-in material resources and authority only when they clearly signal such manifestations of a modern polity. For example, the Western state—especially in post-colonial settings—must show a capacity to set aside ascriptive forms of status and opportunity. Mass opportunity and more just paths of mobility must be signaled. Here the

15

individual is awarded certain entitlements, like schooling, that allegedly ensure upward mobility based upon merit and performance. Of course, certain class interests are served as the state, not village authorities, defines what forms of socialization, language, and knowledge are important. The legitimacy of political elites to engage in such otherwise obtrusive action is set by worldwide expectations of the what the modern Western state is supposed to do, particularly by the ideals and modern social rules that transform polities and economies.

The Western state's implicit agenda can certainly be bumped in self-serving directions by, and for the benefit of, economic elites. But the fragile state must show more versatility to maintain balance and to reinforce its legitimacy. The currency employed—political signals of institution-building, national integration, economic change, and mass opportunity—must resonate to deeply embedded, popular expectation about what the modern state must deliver as it arrives and emerges within disparate Third World societies. Expectations of the state and this currency of political action spread beyond the interests of economic elites. Here I draw on the recent work of John W. Meyer, Francisco Ramirez, John Boli, and their colleagues.[18]

To bolster its own institutional position and boundaries the state must address two distinct environments. First, the state must *draw-in* economic resources and accumulate social capital from its environment. Fragile states typically operate in poor economic environments; at least, popular expectations for "modern progress" far outpace the economic means necessary for delivering on these promises. This constrains political actors' capacity to build the array of institutions held so sacred within the Western conception of polity: efficient organizations of production and exchange, and institutions that construct and enforce social rules about child socialization and fair paths of opportunity. But unless the fragile state can demonstrate progress in building institutions, or even symbolic representations of them, its authority will decline.

When the state *reaches out* to build new institutions, or to co-opt old ones, a second environment is encountered. Similar to the drawing-in of material resources and social authority, outward extension of the state's boundaries through institution-building requires expenditure of material and symbolic resources (See Fig. 1.1). The earliest modern states—the decentralized North American and centralized French regimes—struggled to accumulate sufficient resources to build more schools.[19] In contemporary African countries, we are seeing the decline of mass schooling as fiscally strapped states can no longer afford to pay

Figure 1.1   The State's Accumulation and Expenditure of
Material and Social Capital (in the education sector)

	Material capital	Social capital
Drawing-in institutions and resources	Incorporating private or church schools into the public sector	Mobilizing ideals of individual child development, meritocratic achievement, or moral virtue (via schooling)
Building new institutions and expending resources	Building new schools, hiring more teachers, buying more instructional materials and inputs	Penetrating rural and urban hinterlands, signalling the social and economic benefits of mass schooling

their teachers or maintain crumbling classrooms.[20] In contemporary Western states, resource scarcities or local resistance also constrains central political actors' efficacy in deepening the school's effects.

The spending of political or *social capital* can be quite risky for fragile states. Social capital refers to the ideology, social obligations, and networks that artful political actors mobilize and mold.[21] Political leaders must conserve their social capital. Reinforcing the state through institution-building often involves novel or plainly unpopular actions. For example, pushing for a change in the language of instruction within village schools is deeply controversial, whether political leaders are moving away from, or reinstituting, the high status colonial language. Similarly, recurring attempts by the central state to incorporate and standardize teacher behavior in diverse local schools involves concerted administrative action which risks undercutting central actors' social authority. Thus in the process of institution-building, political actors must carefully pick their targets and selectively apply symbolic measures. Given the shortage of economic resources, Third World leaders often emphasize those institutions that efficiently signal a bundle of modern ideals but which cost relatively little—such as expanding low-quality mass schooling.

The central state's early publicist, Emile Durkheim, understood the pragmatic difficulties associated with mobilizing government's symbolic resources to legitimate France's disparate and mediocre village schools.

More recently, French structuralists have outlined how the state's symbolic actions aim to rationalize economic and civic life.[22] Yet little thought has been given to the difficulties and dilemmas faced by political elites as they struggle to signal modern progress in the face of scarce economic resources, limited technical know-how, and local institutional resistance. We will come back to this issue.

The state's capacity to manage its interdependencies with these two environments reflects its strength or "relative autonomy." I argue that state strength is highly situational, depending upon the diversity and competition among organizations within each environment. To be strong, the state must effectively draw-in material resources and authority from the first institutional environment. Then, the fragile state must act upon its second environment, building new institutions or absorbing old ones into its civic jurisdiction. These two environments vary dramatically (across societies) in terms of competing institutions' levels of authority and resources relative to the state. And state institutions vary in terms of their internal material, administrative, and symbolic capacity to manage interdependencies with these surrounding organizations.

3. Energizing the State's Interdependencies

The diffusion of state authority and agency within Third World societies is like the spread of blue-jeans. The nationalist state arrives expressing universal (Western) ideals, symbols, and organization. Yet, as local crafting and manufacture quickly takes hold, the basic form suddenly sprouts tailored pockets, stitching, and novel shades of blue. When first penetrating a new country, blue-jeans seem peculiar and odd, except among young elites who desire symbolic affiliation with modern fashions. Yet over time blue-jeans become a popular signal of individual modernity among working people, the middle class, even among hip peasant farmers.

The metaphor's validity is limited. For example, blue-jeans have gained far more legitimacy than has the fragile state. Indeed from the grassroots looking up, the Third World state appears as a *particularistic* form, starkly diverging from the social rules inherent in local villages, indigenous forms of production, and local churches.[23] Domestic and foreign political elites, including international agencies, implicitly accept the Western state's presence and authority. But many local people in the Third World do not.

Political analyst Joel Migdal argues that *many Third World societies remain much stronger than their fragile states.* Expectations and demands on the state to deliver economic and social progress are enormous. Also, symbols of state penetration into even remote communities are widespread, including the appearance of a one-room schoolhouse, health clinic, or shack housing the civil magistrate's office. But the state's strength in terms of extracting resources, changing local forms of production, or reordering social practices rarely matches popular expectations. Even when indigenous communities desire change and development, they may resist the means and incursions exercised by the central state. Persistently high rates of fertility and low rates of literacy are two clear examples of the state's limited capacity to actually touch local behavior and cultural commitments. [24]

State actors, struggling to look less particularistic and intrusive, must nurture interdependent alliances with other institutions. Otherwise, they risk a decline in their already tentative authority. Competing institutions are constantly vying for authority and resources presently held within the civic sphere. Support for privatizing state-held enterprises, which have grown since post-colonial days, is a ripe example. The rise of Islamic schools throughout many regions of the world offers another case of the secular state losing control over important elements of civic life.

The state's faith in achieving mass opportunity and equity through nation-wide *corporate* agencies represents an enormous contradiction in Western ideals. One the one hand, the central state holds authority to establish rights and rules of opportunity for the *individual*. The individual's status is no longer determined by the local village, family, or church. The reified individual holds a direct, codified link with the state. Yet modern forms of socialization, employment, and civic participation are organized through secular bureaucracies which are designed to treat everyone identically according to universal routines (that is, "equitably"). The individual allegedly can *achieve* variable levels of economic well-being and status, and is no longer trapped in castes or ascribed forms of status. But the individual (and local collectives) must surrender to the bureaucratic encasement and social rules within which merit must be demonstrated. This, in turn, leads to allocation of material rewards and status that signal "opportunity" and mobility in the Western polity. This bureaucratic form of mass civic life, and its incursion into economic activity, flies in the face of neo-classical and romantic ideals regarding individual freedom, achievement, and market incentives.[25]

This contradiction is stark in African societies. Here fragile states have encountered Western ideals of polity and economy quite late. So, political leaders struggle to catch up, pushing institutions and symbols that signal the coming of mass, meritocratic opportunity. Looking modern brings affection from larger Western states and spurs the arrival of foreign capital. And by signaling the coming of economic growth, real or illusory, the fragile state strengthens its own domestic position.

Yet the building of national institutions, such as mass schooling, requires the incorporation of disparate tribes and language groups into the modern polity and economy. This requires enormous economic and social capital. Political elites usually come from one or two dominant tribes who then draw on secular symbols—embedded in accepted features of the Western state—to broaden their nation-wide authority over other ethnic groups. These subjugated groups fail to see how "mass opportunity" and "national integration" will serve their local forms of authority, socialization, production and exchange.

Marxist theorists might reasonably claim that this is simply an example of class imposition, where political elites advance their core economic and cultural interests against those of peripheral groups. But note that the fragile state must, at the very least, *signal* mass opportunity and national integration. Delivering on the promise of economic growth and greater social well-being requires more rationalized, *nation-wide* organization of firms and state organizations. The large national project of rationalization—of both the economic and social facets of the civic sphere—is led by the state, and is deeply rooted in Western ideals of individual merit and opportunity. Dominant elites may delimit the language, content, and organizations that are advanced during this long term process of rationalization or "national development." But even a small circle of elites must enact the signals and material aspects of *mass* opportunity and merit. Otherwise they will not *look like* a modern state.[26]

Since Third World states entered the network of Western polities quite late, highly centralized agencies must be employed to catch up, to hurry up development. Eager states attempt to quickly rationalize economic production, distribute basic commodities, deliver health services, and socialize children in school. Strict regulation by the central state, of course, exacerbates the foreign and instrusive appearance of political elites as seen through the local villager's eyes.

Against this backdrop, the village school is a relatively unobtrusive and inexpensive device for advancing the state's conception of socialization and mass opportunity. Central states often work with local town councils, village leaders, and churches in expanding and standardizing mass schooling. Under otherwise autocratic Third World states, local councils and district education offices often hold significant authority. These interdependencies at the grassroots are essential in legitimizing the secular school and in motivating local groups to help finance classroom construction. The school often fails to provide children with even basic literacy, offering no real chance for achieving higher status. But the state, collaborating with local elites, *signals* the provision of opportunity and equity. In turn, this process enhances the legitimacy and authority of traditional local leaders who now align themselves with the central state.

4. Methods of Action, Structure, and Individual Agency

Reinforcing and reproducing itself, the state accumulates material and social capital. The state must inhale these essential resources if it is to act with sufficient authority, to build modern institutions. Then, the state acts upon society, molding and reinforcing the rules that govern the economy and polity.[27] By focusing on the expansion and deepening of mass schooling, I explore one case of how the Western state draws-in and expends material capital and social legitimacy.

Third World states have great difficulty in playing out their (interdependent) rocky romance with the school. Political elites must rush to deliver on promises of mass opportunity. Yet the state's material resources are limited, and its political authority is often quite shaky. Given these conditions, the central state often imposes a structure that *appears* to be uniform and strictly regulated: central education ministries set a standard curriculum, encourage teachers to simply drill these "facts" into the heads of children, then rigidly test children on memorization of these bits of knowledge. Fragile, resource-poor states also employ highly centralized administrative practices. Tight administrative control is rarely realized, particularly when the majority of teachers are in far-flung rural areas, infrequently visited by the lone school inspector. But centralized administrative methods at least signal that modern, corporate forms of organization are being employed. Political elites believe that basic control of the school institution will be maintained. And will not pupil achievement rise as modern school management is tightened? Some political leaders do realize that material resources and administrative controls are scarce or ineffective. Then, states and political actors resort to symbolic action and argument.

In sum, I pursue two basic questions about these *three* forms of state action—the allocation of material resources, administrative practices, and symbolic expressions. First, when and how is each method of influence exercised by the fragile Third World state? Second, do these methods really act to *structure* the behavior and belief of local school actors, or is individual agency still available? Certainly, the state has efficaciously built and reinforced the mass school's legitimacy and popularity. But how is the state doing in its struggle to deepen the school's effects? Chapters 2 and 3 address these issues with regard to central states. Chapter 4 takes us inside African schools and classrooms, to look at the form and (questionable) efficacy of the state's methods for controlling local action.

The state's desire to intensify, or recast, the structure of the local school is shaped by its interdependencies with its institutional environment.[28] The amount of local agency allowed by the state depends upon political elites' own level of agency, that is, their own relative autonomy. States in very poor societies, illustrated throughout Africa, must rush to look modern, to provide mass opportunity, to standardize the system of merit and mobility. Ironically, popular demands placed on the state encourage the erosion of local agency and pluralistic social rules. The central state must incorporate and standardize local schooling, since this signals modern progress. In contrast, middle-income states, such as South Korea or Mexico, hold greater material resources and legitimacy. The uniform and autocratic form of school organization begins to loosen as the maturing polity is no longer satisfied with *symbols* of mass opportunity. Here more varied strategies emerge for boosting educational quality and deepening the school's effects.

The environment or institutional structures within which the state operates also change over historical stretches of time. Young economic firms and stable markets may be coalescing; differentiated social classes and communities may be forming; a nation-wide language and system of merit or status solidifies; the relative power of different political elites, ethnic groups, and classes may be shifting. Indeed the fragile state is earnestly trying to hurry change in its environment—toward economic rationalization, cultural integration, and bureaucratic forms of work and civic life. Of course, political elites seek these institutional changes in ways that minimally disrupt their own authority and advantage. Yet the unsettling reality remains: the state's surrounding environment changes over time, and political actors must adjust their interdependencies to backstop their popular legitimacy and to expand their resources.

Summary

This book attempts to paint the complex Western state on a small canvass. State actors' attempts at influencing other institutions and individuals are fairly easy to sketch within the textured foreground. But the backdrop is a shifting sea of strong contextual forces—from ideologies to well-defined organizations—that push and pull at the fragile state. These background factors often appear with all the fuzziness of an impressionist painting. Yet if we are to grasp the motivations, methods, and erratic effects of state actors, we must ask these surrounding forces to hold still.

This introductory chapter has outlined the double-edged problem confronting fragile Third World states—the dilemma of expanding mass education while struggling to deepen the school's actual effects. This contradictory agenda has enormous practical implications, stretching the state's fiscal resources and popular credibility. It also provides a colorful case of how state actors struggle to signal modern progress and mass opportunity, independent of whether their efforts yield significant local effects. The state weaves its way through a treacherous institutional environment filled with uncertainties and exigencies. Relentless popular expectations push the state to build more schools, despite government's limited material capacity to ensure minimal levels of educational quality. High levels of administrative uncertainty prompt more centralized controls and symbolic action, yet fail to materially deepened the school's effects.

As the political actors struggle with external ambiguities, then try alternative methods of cajoling local schools, a novel image of the fragile state comes into focus. The state is best seen as a bounded institution but one that must respond to a mix of interests and interdependencies. It behaves much like a small firm, searching for a warm market niche and a set of sturdy institutional foundations. The state mobilizes ideals and symbols, as well as acquiring material capital and technical know-how, as it fights for popular legitimacy and organizational efficacy. As a part of this process, the state looks laterally to its institutional neighbors, drawing-in their resources and political support. The state also looks downward to weaker organizations, like the local school, which it can co-opt and use as a stage for playing out the signals of modernity.

We will look into the state's motivations, sources of political energy, and resulting forms of influence that are attempted (whether effective or not). This also brings us back to contradictions: the Western tension between individual development and bureaucratic forms of merit and opportunity; the tension between unceasing urban demands placed on young states versus the resilient societies and ethnic communities that resist or simply ignore political elites; and conflict between the Western state's need to acquire more economic capital while preaching the need for individual initiative, novel (modern) social behavior, and the atomized pursuit of individual opportunity. The fragile state is energized not so much by a clear sense of purpose and coherent ideals, as by the threatening demands and political batterings which stem from these contradictions.

2

What Drives the Expansion and Deepening of Mass Schooling?

Individual actors do not invent and bolster the rules that define how "modern children" grow up—institutions do. Let's step back from the state institution for a moment and gaze more widely across the organizational landscape within which it is situated. Keep in mind *the* pragmatic questions facing policymakers, educators, and local leaders: How can the pace of school expansion be quickened? How can the school's effects on children be intensified?

The state is simply one player within the Western polity's broad effort to formally socialize its children. Wider forces, moving independently of political elites, may eclipse the state's attempts to expand and deepen mass education. Demands placed on children to work—in the home, in the fields, or on the street—exemplify how local economic and cultural factors constrain the state's influence (in the Third World). In addition, we need to grasp how deeply ingrained ideological and economic forces, originating outside the state apparatus but linked to Western ideals regarding the individual and the political-economy, shape political elites' fervent advocacy of mass schooling.

This chapter backs up to review earlier thinking and recent evidence on how diverse institutions can drive the *expansion* of mass schooling. I review three competing theories which take into account demands pressed by several institutions, including the family, economy, church, and state, not to mention the school institution's own bullish desire to spawn itself. These frameworks—functional modernization, class imposition, and world institution theories—continue to shape our everyday beliefs about why mass schooling is important within Western polities, and which institutions do (or should) push educational expansion. The three theories, at times, also offer explanations for the state's attempt to *deepen* the school's effect.

Much has been already written on these theories. I do not aim to simply add another detailed review. Instead, I focus on their sharply contrasting representations of (a) the institutional environment that encircles the state, (b) how these surrounding institutions energize and constrain the action of political elites, and (c) how the state's determined romance with the school advances the interests of certain groups. I start with a brief overview, then proceed to a more critical discussion of each theory. Recent empirical evidence is then discussed which challenges the universal claims of each grand theory. This brings us back to a picture of the fragile state that recognizes *variation in institutional environments* across societies and historical periods, variation which sets conditions that enhance or constrain the state's capacity to boost mass schooling and to deepen its effects on children.

Three Stories Introduced

Western advocates of *modernization* make two central arguments. First, secular nation-wide institutions must be constructed to replace local collectives and ethnic affiliations, manifest in village, church, and family units. Cooperation on a national scale—expressed through universal language, forms of merit and mobility, markets, and corporate organization—will serve sacred commitments to economic growth and to stable political organizations. Second, the individual, when detached from traditional local authority and fused to the secular state, will be motivated to serve national commitments. Mass schooling is the instrument that socializes children toward central authority and modern affiliations. Indeed, one common indicator of a nation's level of modernity is the school enrollment rate—the proportion of children and adults who have swallowed this medicine called mass schooling.

Critics of Western education do not disagree with the modernists' portrayal of the school institution's functional role. But this concerted action of central and local elites is interpreted as a process of *class imposition*. Political elites are seen as pushing the language, knowledge, and sacred customs of their particular tribe or subculture. And elites, whether located in the state or the economy, have the most to gain by eroding or co-opting competing forms of local authority and exchange. Class imposition theorists also look at school-level rules and knowledge, emphasizing the factory-like organization of mass schooling. Here hierarchical forms of power and work are advanced, the child must achieve along standardized and universal criteria, and knowledge is reduced to easily testable bits of information. Schooling functionally prepares children to pursue merit and mobility in mass organizations.

Most recently, modernist and class imposition explanations have been challenged from a third perspective—a less materialist *institutional* theory of how schools expand and deepen. World institution theorists emphasize that the historical rise of mass schooling corresponded (in Europe) to the emergence of the secular state. In addition, school expansion in most polities has occurred independently of economic forces, discounting functionalist claims apparent in earlier models of modernization. Instead, the legitimacy and utility of mass schooling is rooted within the West's conception of the state as reproduced by institutionalized expectations of the political apparatus. To build popular support within a nation, and to establish status within the Western interstate network, political elites must express certain ideals and goals. Here the school as an institution holds enormous symbolic value within the Western state's logic. The school is not necessarily required to serve economic interests. The institution is simply an expressive form, employed by political elites to signal modern progress and reinforce the state structure.

World institution theory resembles the work of European structuralists, emphasizing how the school serves as an institutional signal of the secular state's ideals and as a device for mediating contradictions inherent within the capitalist state. Yet world institution proponents presume a greater degree of popular acceptance of the school, challenging the Marxist contention that states act to *impose* certain ideals, institutions, and economic forms. World institution theorists even ask whether the school is really part of the state, or is instead a broad-based social movement which determines its own internal social rules, forms of legitimate knowledge, and indicators of merit and status.

Institutional theorists question whether the state's attempt to deepen the school's effects are efficacious, particularly when it relies on mechanical administrative action. Building from Emile Durkheim's original insights, institutionalists argue that the state constructs schools and controls curricula as a strategy for extending membership in the modern polity. Cohesion of the school organization depends not, however, on factory-like administration but on a shared commitment to certain rituals expressing membership. For instance, when African kids sit each day in crumbling thatch-roof classrooms, and teachers lecture at them for hours on end, these are rituals that signal who holds power over the socialization of children. Very little may actually be learned. But the

27

state and its central institution—the school—gain enormous authority. Parents and children are signaling membership ritualistically in the modern polity. It is this symbol-filled harmonizing between state and school that helps unify and homogenize the cohering polity. Yet since the school itself is bounded, complex, and highly institutionalized, its romance with the state may be quite rocky.

Contrasting Dimensions of Competing Theories

Next, I detail each of the three models. You might think critically about each theory, particularly in their contrasting interpretations of the Western state's *motivations, methods of influence, and actual effects.* My review emphasizes the following facets of each model. First, like any human organization, the state is motivated by its own ideals *and* by its interdependencies with surrounding institutions. The three theories differ on the degree of autonomy that can be exercised by actors within the state organization, including their capacity to buffer or challenge the interests of surrounding institutions. Current theory and empirical research, for instance, emphasize the influence of economic growth and labor demand on school expansion, not the independent force of the state. Second, the models differ in their descriptions and interpretations of how the state acts to expand *and* deepen schooling. This leap across levels of analysis—the state's institution-level action linked to expansion versus strategies aimed at classroom-level effects—is a treacherous jump. The theories vary in the care taken in distinguishing antecedent forces and processes that unfold within each of these two levels. Third, my review includes evidence on the state's actual effects. Putting these three basic models to empirical tests, although slow in coming, has helped push theory toward more defensible and useful representations.

These theories engage in *description* and *interpretation* of action by various institutions: the state, economic firms, local labor structures, churches, and the family. The theories focus on different causal events and mediating processes. Even when looking at the same event, competing theories often assign different meanings. The models vary on the level of *resistance and conflict* that is likely to erupt between local groups and central elites (be they economic, political, or religious leaders). Relatedly, the three theories differ on the *role and power of elites* within emerging polities. Do elites deterministically *impose* their moral and economic ideals on the masses? Or do the symbols and material improvements associated with "national development" lead the unquestioning masses to take the sacraments of modernity and internalize Western commitments?

Theory 1—Functionalist Modernity

Our images of being modern stem from the fusion of economic ideals and revolutionary realities which unfolded in the late eighteenth century. The liberal state's rise in North America, then in France, helped to legitimate key beliefs associated with modernity. Of particular importance here, the reified construct of the "autonomous individual" was balanced against the task of pulling together a unified republic, as these fledgling states eagerly tried to incorporate disparate individuals into a nation-wide consciousness and political structure. The sacred individual was crafted ideologically by bounding the state's control over mercantile economic activity. But this liberal shift also stigmatized the individual's traditional economic and communal bonds to feudal, church, and village authorities. Emerging political elites argued that this realignment of individual loyalty toward the nation-state was necessary, essentially providing new institutional foundations and a secular cosmology within which capitalist markets could flourish. Of course, looking up from the local collective, the secular state and its bureaucratic agencies appeared and continue to appear rather particularistic and foreign.[1]

Closely following this revolution in how the liberal state constructed the individual, came the industrial revolution. The industrial firm gained enormous legitimacy. The corporate form of cooperation proved enormously effective in economic terms—at least for some. The industrial firm was characterized by hierarchical authority, magical technology and science, standardization of both material and human "systems," and reliance upon extrinsic material rewards for work performance. Mass production brought rising levels of wealth and consumption (the latter resulting from lower prices for mass produced goods). Thus the industrial bureaucracy took on enormous credibility as a symbol of modernization and economic change. Even today, when political leaders and educators talk about "modernizing schools" or "improving school effectiveness" they usually envision bureaucratic ways of organizing—sharpening lines of authority, subdividing labor into more routinized (teaching or administrative) tasks, standardizing what is learned, and tightening evaluation of uniform knowledge and action.[2]

Contemporary functionalists—be they activists or scholars—emphasize how the Western state can *socialize* the individual to adopt modern forms of work, social relations, and moral ideals.[3] The sixteenth-century British state, for instance, dissolved the rights of feudal clans to own and control the use of land; instead, the liberal state constructed a legal structure to allow individual ownership and inheritance of property. Early Western states also enacted liberal employment statutes, yielding a "free" labor force of individuals who were no longer obliged to remain with a particular landlord or village.[4] Such interventions by political elites into the economy reflected both a popular ideological commitment to individual entitlements, as well as a response to nascent capitalists seeking a more flexible labor force.

Contemporary states, both within industrialized and Third World nations, construct and reinforce ideals and institutions that legitimate certain forms of economic action. We can observe a United States president allowing the consolidation of firms into larger and larger conglomerates; or we can see a socialist African president financing farmer cooperatives in the countryside. In both cases the central state (and political elites within) are functionally defining what legitimate economic activity entails and building concrete organizations which embody their economic ideals. Fragile states, operating in post-colonial polities, often face pre-modern economic structures. Political elites must respond to, and gain credibility with, private firms that dominate certain sectors (usually exporters of raw materials and agricultural products). Or the political apparatus directly controls parastatal firms. In both cases, the introduction of liberal rules regarding markets, property, and commercial rights is a politically difficult process, effecting the economic power of elites and prices facing both urban residents and rural peasants.

A State-Defined Common Good?

Universal economic rules become credible only when the formal polity is unified by shared cultural understandings—manifest in a common language, sacred symbols, and social rules that have broad currency.[5] Functionalists see the secular state as the pivotal actor in breaking down cultural differences and in defining "the common good." By constructing and legitimating civic institutions—schools, health centers, rule-making organizations—the state hopes to integrate heretofore balkanized tribes.

Fragile Third World states are continually fighting this battle. Historically, dual economic structures have operated within most post-colonial societies. At one level, rural subsistence farmers live off their own crops, taking a fraction of their surplus produce to the local market. Yet in the wage sector, large-scale mining, agricultural, and manufacturing firms produce for urban elites and for export markets. This bifurcated economy leads to persistent political pressure for—under the Western state's own logic—integrating caste-like groups, building a meritocratic system of opportunity, and broadening access to urban-based goods and symbols of modernity. The legitimacy of state actors comes to depend upon their ability to integrate peripheral tribes or subcultures into more modern institutions. This leads to demands on the state to construct Western-like institutions and to extend membership in the modern (urban) polity to the masses. The state, given its vital commitment to national integration, then defines the language, customs, forms of work and institutional participation that signify status within the modern polity.

Similarly, when industrialized Western polities face economic downturns or sharp cultural division, heads of state redouble their pleas for society to pull together—to work harder and to resist ideological conflict among local "tribes" (be they ethnic or class groups, political parties, or formal organizations competing for capital and popular legitimacy). Political elites also scramble to reinforce, or adjust, institutional rules. The United States' declining stature in the world economy, for instance, continues to prompt an odd array of educational reforms: new schools focused on teaching math and science, tightening up on what teachers teach, restrictions on what languages can be spoken in the classroom. Note that underlying these attempts to reinforce the school institution is a concern that plural groups must be more tightly corralled into a more homogeneous polity.

Balancing The State's Romantic Instincts

Contradicting the state's integrative agenda is its romantic liberal side. Rejecting the historically centralized authority of the Catholic

Church, feudal lords, and mercantilist monarchs, early secular theorists saw the state as the great legitimizer and protector of the individual's newly constructed rights. Just as Protestant sects, rising after the Reformation, advocated a direct link between God and the individual, secular theorists argued that the state should protect and embellish the individual *citizen.*[6] In one way, this romantic recasting of the individual as holding autonomy, freedom, and self-interested rationality did not contradict the state's integrative function. The rising middle class of merchants, artisans, and professionals saw individual liberty as instrumental to advancing their own economic interests. But the individual's new-found, romantic capacity for political and expressive freedom (within secular bounds) was, and continues to be, at odds with the Western state's interest in homogenizing plural communities.

The school is uniquely positioned as the institutional fulcrum that balances these contradictory ideological commitments expressed by the state. Liberal political elites are under enormous pressure to advance the individual's developmental interests. Simultaneously, it must try to incorporate diverse communities into a unified nation. Given the state's interest in political and economic stability, the school becomes a relatively inexpensive mechanism for balancing these tension-ridden ideals. The state accomplishes this ideological balancing act through three strategies.

First, the expansion of mass schooling and its association with modern progress serves to de-legitimate what John Boli and his colleagues term, *intermediate collectives.* Historically, children were socialized by their parents, kin, and within their local village church. But these collective units, operating between the individual and the state, can subvert the state's direct influence on the child. Just as missionaries once brought religion to "uncivilized lands," the liberal state brings secular faith, sacred symbols, and direct membership in the state-defined polity and wage economy. Loyalty to local interests is of the wrong scale. Individuals, to act modern, must display affection for economic and social institutions that operate on a national scale. Expanding access to mass schooling and intensifying implementation of a standardized national curriculum exemplify how the state earnestly extends nation-level membership and universally defined (modern) status to the child.[7]

Second, the state attempts to construct a nation-wide opportunity structure, standard forms of merit, and concrete strategies for gaining status in adulthood. Once Western social rules penetrate a territory, state actors risk losing popular legitimacy if methods for allocating status, work, and income seem unfair and closed. The persistence of ascriptive forms of status and kin-based power structures sharply undercuts state actors' legitimacy over time. The mass school helps define a common meritocratic order where each individual child appears to have a fair chance at getting ahead— *if* he or she works hard and learns how to achieve within modern (bureaucratic) organizations. In classically liberal polities the construct of technical "skill" is closely attached to "opportunity." Adult status is not determined by caste or class membership but by one's persistence in learning skills which are interwoven with normative forms of language, dress, and custom. This is functional for the nation-state, since productivity, material accumulation, and hence the state's own stability depend both on a broad division of labor and popular perception that the opportunity structure is fair.

Mechanisms linked to the allocation of status and opportunity are critical elements of national education systems. These organizational devices are far more important than whether any learning actually occurs in the classroom. National examinations in Africa, for instance, often contain questions and information which never appear within textbooks or the national curriculum. The content or relevance of the exam is not important from political elites' point of view. What *is* important is that the examination process appear to be fair and credible, as the mechanism for sorting youths into scarce secondary school places and thus into better jobs. The extreme case, common in anglophone Africa, is where secondary school pupils sit for national examinations modeled after the colonial Cambridge exams. The content of the test has little relevance to the content of African curricula, not to mention knowledge that might be useful in a Third World setting. But the exam itself holds enormous status and legitimacy as a sorting mechanism.

Third, the Western state instinctively expresses a moral belief that the individual's own capacities and quality of life can be bettered by formal institutions. Under the modern state, we come to believe that socialization of children only by parents or the local community is insufficient in developing the child's potential. A state-constructed bureaucratic institution—the school—can best nurture the child's inner resources. In the process the child will come to realize the nation's "common good" and contribute to the polity's shared interests. That is, the formal school will strengthen the child's membership in, and affiliation with, the modern state, placing emotional loyalty to the local village or tribe in the (properly) subordinate position.[8] Throughout the popular press in the Third World, national leaders recurrently urge parents and village chiefs to keep their children in school. Commonly, political elites cite two reasons for why traditional hesitancy about government schooling should be overcome: the child's individual development, and how this form of education fits the agenda of national development. Importantly, the literacy, knowledge, and social skills which the child gains at school are *not* linked to the welfare of family or village. True to Rousseau, Jefferson, and Durkheim, when the child grows up modern, he or she is being inducted into the larger scale project of *national* development.

Theory 2—Class Imposition

Since the 1960s, of course, the functionalist-modernity framework has been sharply challenged by scholars, activists, and even by a few political leaders who see the Western state's agenda less innocently. These critics agree that the state seeks to control how children are socialized, using the school to fit the modernized youth into a secular polity populated by bureaucratic organizations and national markets. Yet, Marxist writers and local activists hold a critical *interpretation* of how this integrative or homogenizing role of the state is acted out—a story-line that involves expansion and deepening of the mass school. Functional theorists see nation-building and formal "child-building" as progressive elements of modernization. In contrast, critical theorists step back and question this process, asking which groups gain and which groups lose social authority and material resources.

Class imposition (or conflict) theorists have highlighted the primacy of *economic interests* inherent in Western polities, not the romantic social ideals rhetorically espoused by the liberal state. The state, as an agent of economic elites, possesses little institutional autonomy and little capacity to pursue social agendas that do not serve the central capitalist project of economic expansion. Here the state simply plays the role of messenger, pressing to ensure that the school socializes children to fit into the goals and social rules of economic firms and markets. In turn the school, as a financially dependent organ of the state, must respond to the demands and material organization of capital, technology, and labor. Both the government and the school are parts of the superstructure that simply sits on top of a foundation of economic interests to which the action of political elites must correspond. From this logic, economic interests drive the expansion and deepening of schooling, with the state serving as a subservient middleman.[9]

The central state's articulation of the common good, according to the class imposition model, actually *reinforces the status, affluence, knowledge, and customs of economic elites.* Indeed, the functionalist-modernity model often reflects an innocent disregard for (a) which particular classes or ethnic tribes dominate economic firms and state agencies, (b) how their interests differ from lower-status groups, and (c) the extent to which state action (intentionally or inadvertently) leads to the reproduction of class divisions and inequality. Critical theorists emphasize how the state acts to conserve class-based differences and inequities, failing to reorder the distribution of wealth and status, and rarely respecting cultural differences held by low-status groups (that is, "low-status" as defined by the dominant ethnic group or economic class).

Class imposition theorists, therefore, make a *coercive interpretation* of the Western state's historical role in rationalizing or harmonizing economic, political, and cultural organizations—moving from plural social groups and rules to a uniform secular polity and nation-wide consciousness. Functionalist writers see the breaking down of local groups and legitimization of secular institutions (like the school) as a sign of modernity—a wise mechanism for pulling the individual into the formal polity and into modern forms of production and exchange. Class theorists see this as an attempt to achieve hegemonic faith in economic expansion, indeed sanctioning material growth as the polity's preeminent moral commitment. By placing high status on working and achieving within bureaucratic organizations, economic elites (via the state) legitimate the way in which their firms organize production. Local tribes and communities may hold other social and economic forms as sacred, be it their languages, gods, or local forms of production and exchange. But such local diversity is anathema to the modern state's desire for solidarity and loyalty to nation-wide institutions and markets. Elites argue that the individual should gain status by joining and achieving within the formal institution (be it a school or a firm). Involvement of local collectives—the family, village, or church—is defined by secular elites as unmodern, possessing low status.

Next I illustrate how these three postulates of class imposition theory—the primacy of economic interests, the reproduction of class differences, and a coercive interpretation of state action—lead to an alternative explanation of why economic and political elites seek to expand and deepen schooling.

Overly Optimistic About the State?

Since the late eighteenth century, elites active in constructing the liberal state have been hopeful about this institution's potential role in pulling together disparate provinces, defining a common cultural agenda, and motivating the individual to develop (and produce). Locke argued that the individual's rights could be legitimated and protected only by a strong state. Divine authoritative law, previously handed down by the church and monarchs, was to be replaced by sacred entitlements granted to each individual by the secular state. Despite his romantic confidence in the natural character of the individual, Rousseau also claimed that only a forceful state could enhance freedom and equality. Through the individual's "social contract" with the state, the individual would participate in the modern polity's common agenda; in return, the state would construct and preserve the individual citizen's civil liberties.[10]

Both Rousseau and, later, Emile Durkheim stressed that ignorance led to passive acceptance of inequality and repression by strong states. Schooling—by socializing new generations to collectively-held ideals and cultural commitments—would better the polity over time. The central state was to provide common schools through which the modern state's secular faith could be transmitted to children. Adam Smith argued that the state should allow individuals to act from a "natural desire" to pursue their own material interests. This collection of atomistic actors, operating within unencumbered markets and free of state regulation, would boost the common good. Yet even Smith believed that cooperation in market exchange was founded upon a "sacred regard to general rules." He went on to say that these "moral faculties . . . were set up within us to be the supreme arbiters of all our actions, to superintend all our senses, passions, and appetites."[11] Even those, like Smith, who emphasized the liberal materialist side of the secular state, urged political elites to define moral rules and influence the socialization of children.[12]

Karl Marx's interpretation of the central state's intent and actions was far more critical, far less optimistic. Two facets of Marx's general perspective are particularly important to the class imposition camp. He argued that the state, in most cases, acts to improve conditions for capitalist expansion. The Western state's utilitarian actions—legitimating and legislating individual rights regarding property, production, labor, and trade—emphasize a strong secular faith in economic growth. But such action is more functional for certain classes than for others.

Marx believed that only in rare instances did the state pursue social policies and exercise moral leadership that was contrary to the interests of economic elites.

Importantly, Marx did observe that the state bureaucracy achieved some organizational independence, since the bourgeoisie disliked involvement in the daily conflicts facing governments. This usually involved political tussles among competing economic organizations. The central state may voice concern over material inequality or social opportunity, but this is motivated by political elites' desire for stability and for reinforcing popular support. In general, the state rarely is distracted from its fundamental role of serving economic elites' obsession with economic expansion.

Marx also argued that state actors would achieve a degree of institutional independence when no particular class was sufficiently organized to dominate other classes. This point holds enormous relevance in Third World countries where state agencies often hold more investment capital and organizational cohesion than do fledgling private firms. This stems from strong historical forces: earlier domination of colonial administrations by economic interests; the nationalist state's subsequent distrust of private, often foreign-held companies; and pre-modern political leaders' desire to share in the profits of key parastatal businesses. Here government leaders—who run social services *and* state-held enterprises—form the elite class. These elites may move independently of pure (private) economic interests, indeed they often discourage liberal competition from domestic or foreign owned firms. Yet state-run enterprises do face pressures to be publicly accountable and appear to serve the ideal of mass participation and opportunity. This is not to say that moral faith in economic expansion is any less in post-colonial polities—simply that many economic elites are located within the state structure, and they frequently must accommodate social goals more so that purely private elites.[13]

State Reinforcement of Class Inequality

Class imposition theorists highlight two important examples of how the state and its school institution construct, then reinforce, an achievement structure which yields unequal opportunity. First, within industrialized countries, schools hold little influence in determining either a child's *relative* level of academic achievement or eventual occupational status, after accounting for his or her parents' social class background. Empirical evidence shows that schools do little to alter the reproduction of a society's (unequal) class structure.[14] This may be due to lower levels of instructional quality in schools attended by low-income kids (although levels of *material* school resources are often equal). Or schools may not be able to overcome advantageous socialization practices exercised by parents of middle and upper class children.[15] Despite the optimistic faith held by Rousseau, Durkheim, and their contemporary disciples, the state is unable to reduce class inequalities. By placing responsibility on the individual child and family—to work hard and compete against fellow pupils within a secular meritocracy—the state structure is not questioned. In fact, the "structure" is barely visible.

A growing empirical literature now indicates that in many Third World societies schooling more effectively levels social class differences. When the class structure is not highly differentiated, schooling does appear to provide mobility to children of rural peasants and the urban poor. The social class background of pupils also influences achievement less in math and subjects that are foreign to indigenous forms of knowledge. In contrast, student achievement in language is more consistently sensitive to class background, rather than variation in school quality. Ironically, as national economies grow and the labor structure becomes more differentiated, labor demand often levels-off for highly schooled youth. The now familiar pattern of credentialism takes hold, whereby more schooling is required simply to remain competitive in a labor queue that grows longer and longer. By this time, the school is highly institutionalized and enrollments rise independent of labor demand. Varation in children's social class background now kicks-in to influence which youth can afford to stay in school for longer periods.[16]

The second example of state-reinforced inequality relates to political and economic leaders' argument (for two centuries now) that mass schooling should do a better job of preparing productive, more conforming young workers. In the United States, for example, business and labor organizations have historically pushed either to expand vocational training programs, or to make the general curriculum more "practical." When corporate leaders face shortages of unskilled factory workers, computer operators, secretaries, or technicians they push the state to train more. In contemporary times, business leaders have focused less on skill training, emphasizing to governments that they simply want young workers who are literate, show up on time, and fit into the bureaucratic rules of production firms. At a deeper level, concern in the

United States over making the economy more competitive encourages civic disdain for curricula and knowledge which are not directly linked to technological progress and productivity. This push to further vocationalize schooling predictably occurs when economic downturns threaten the state's popular support. Under this condition, political elites must strengthen their interdependencies with economic interests.

In sum, the dominant class—residing in state and economic organizations—emphasize the moral project of economic expansion. Especially within fragile states, both the illusion and reality of mass opportunity depend upon material growth. Schooling instrumentally provides the vocational skills and technical mind-set seemingly required to spur material growth. Yet despite efforts to expand and deepen mass education, class theorists argue that the school institution is not effective in improving the *distribution* of achievement and income. The school may project the institutional illusion of more equal opportunity; but it really does not threaten the relative dominance of incumbent elites according to class imposition theorists. We will return to this question shortly when we review the empirical evidence.

The State's Push for a Bureaucratic Moral Order

Critical scholars (especially European structuralists) emphasize a still deeper means of influence exercised by the state. Mass schooling not only attempts to instruct technical skills necessary for economic productivity and expansion. The state also formulates a "hidden curriculum" to transmit the basic attitudes and rules upon which civil society and mass organization are founded. Samuel Bowles and Herbert Gintis, for example, argued that schools in the United States were expanded during the industrial revolution to control and socialize errant immigrant youth, teaching them English, vocational skills, and a conception of time and regimen manifest both in bureaucratic schools and firms.[17]

Robert Dreeben, though not a class imposition theorist, digs deeper into the social mores of North American classrooms. He shows how very young children are taught to discard personalized (or particularistic) forms of evaluation and, instead, are pushed to internalize universal forms of behavior and achievement based on standardized pieces of knowledge. Despite being treated in uniform ways in mass schools, children are taught that they can gain status by working autonomously and competing against their classmates. Teachers implicitly socialize children to see the utility of this secular faith in hard work and individualistic achievement.

Yet these basic rules for getting ahead are embedded within a hierarchical bureaucratic organization. The Calvinist commitment to self-righteous hard work—originally pushed in North America by church leaders, self-reliant farmers, and later by entrepreneurial industrialists—continues to be reproduced within the first mass, corporate institution encountered by the child. Dreeben sees this "hidden curriculum" as a manifestation of implicit rules that operate in broader Western culture, not of a curricular agenda rationally assembled by elites. The mass school does set the context and achievement structure within which individualistic virtues are acted out. Then the state claims that opportunity flows from the individual's own effort, since the school apparently treats every child the same and recognizes merit in uniform ways.[18]

Class imposition theorists argue that the modern state mobilizes mass schooling to sanctify the knowledge and implicit social rules upon which the Western polity and bureaucratic organization are founded. Antonio Gramsci, an Italian socialist writing in the 1920s, argued that the liberal state rarely exercises physical coercion or obtrusive imposition of class interests. Instead the state's strength lies in its more subtle ability to ensure "the acceptance by the ruled of a conception of the world which belongs to the rulers." The mass school, as argued above, transmits the message that the burden is on the individual. The child must work hard if he or she wants to get ahead. The *structure* through which the young person moves disappears from sight—deeply institutionalized in the polity and implicitly accepted as legitimate, neutral, and fair.[19]

Gramsci, in general, backed Marx's view of the state as a centralized and coercive agency. Yet he introduced two theoretical departures. First, Gramsci highlighted the potency of ideology and social institutions, relative to obtrusive regulation by state or economic elites. Second, he focused on conflict arising between a central state seeking popular support and ideological hegemony, versus a pluralistic polity divided by centrifugal social forces. Marx held a deterministic view that economic elites simply manipulated the central state to reinforce conservative institutions and ideals. Gramsci agreed that the dominant class *attempts* to imprint their conception of reality and their moral (economic) commitments onto subordinate classes. Yet such attempts at class imposition often are met with indifference or outright resistance—especially when elite actors' beliefs are viewed as illegitimate "ideology" rather than as institutionalized "common sense." This conflict was painfully clear to

Gramsci as his popular socialist party first combatted, then lost working-class members to Mussolini's fascist party. At other times, reproduction of dominant ideology can occur unabated through explicit political persuasion or via more subtle institutions, such as through mass schooling.

Recent research within schools emphasizes that obtrusive *imposition* of dominant class interests is rarely observed. Teachers and schools, however, do gently impress a certain order. High achieving students are easy. They are buying into, and feeling efficacious within, the classroom's underlying social rules and moral order as described by Dreeben. On the other hand, students who fail to perform within the school's official structure resist or simply choose to evade and exit from the dominant order.

Robert Everhart's year-long study within one junior secondary school reveals that *conflicts* arise daily between poor achieving youth and their teachers (the front-line agents of the school's formal structure). These pupils fail to engage the curriculum, the knowledge, and symbols valued by the teacher. They may not perform within the social rules established by the teacher; they may ally themselves with other youth in actively resisting the teacher's authority. But Everhart emphasizes that the teacher's classroom rules and sanctified knowledge are rarely driven down the throats of (or imposed upon) dissonant students. These kids simply detach from the school's rules for how to achieve. When direct conflicts do arise, the non-performing student, of course, loses the battle. Over time the student fades from serious engagement within the classroom, subtly becoming disenfranchised from the school's official structure. This process of disenfranchisement preserves the school's social order and dominant class interests, at least to the extent that these are represented in the classroom's curriculum and bureaucratic social rules. Yet reinforcement of the social order occurs *not* through imposition but rather through smooth handling of class-related conflict.[20]

The State as Independent Mediator?

Marx argued that economic elites either captured positions of political authority or simply strong-armed state actors. This presumption of correspondence between economic interests and state action is increasingly questioned by both adherents to and critics of class imposition theory. Louis Althusser, for one, suggests that state expansion is explained not by the *harmony* between economic and political leaders (as functionalists claim), but instead due to recurrent *conflict* between dominant classes and the masses (or the rising bourgeoisie) who have tired of persistent inequality or unliberal economic constraints. State construction of mass schooling, for instance, paints an institutional backdrop against which each individual appears to have an equal shot at getting ahead. The state broadens its popular legitimacy by breaking down ascriptive determinants of success (such as, kin, tribal, ethnic, or gender connections). In their stead, the state sanctions institutions and social rules that ensure impersonal, nation-wide forms of merit. For children, these modern forms of achievement and character are operationalized by the state within the institution of mass schooling. In so doing, the state mediates and cools-out conflict between advantaged elites and groups struggling to enlarge their economic and social status.[21]

The institutions of state and school may gain some independence and running room *if* they hold sufficient political capital. The boundaries confining the state's action also become elastic when the dominant economic class loses its grip on the state. Yet the legitimacy of state and school remain dependent upon political actors' capacity to mobilize liberal goals and modern symbols—signals of the state's promise to boost material welfare, equalize access to material goodies, and expand institutional memberships that confer higher status (like the school). These comprise the currency through which political actors mediate class conflicts. Only political elites who desire early retirement dare to argue against economic expansion or oppose individualistic conceptions of rights and economic action. I will return to the dynamic ways in which the state and the school each struggle to gain institutional autonomy. Here the essential point put forward by the European structuralists is that highly legitimated ideology, reproduced in formal institutions, set the parameters beyond which central elites or local activists can not move. Individual violators—including dissonant or impassive students—are not necessarily coerced into conforming. They simply are disenfranchised and never pulled-in to benefit from the modern polity's relatively lucrative opportunity structure.

State Signals of Modern Organization

The institutionalized acceptance of bureaucratic social rules, values, and symbols of modern socialization within North American schools is particularly instructive.[22] Actual administration of United States schools is highly decentralized; the central government plays a small (and cheap) role relative to the codified authority and resources of state and local governments. Despite this high level of "local control," what actually goes on in classrooms across the United States is remarkably uniform: children progress through standard grade levels, all hearing the same sacred pieces of vocabulary, arithmetic, and homogenized history; and all instructed by teachers who rely on similar pedagogical practices, lecturing at children, handing out dittos, often forming "ability-based" groups for some lessons. This surprising similarity in schooling across a very diverse society stems, in part, from the institution's own independence and self-contained culture.

This uniformity also is rooted in the ideological and political strength of dominant elites and in the incorporation of their culture into fledgling agencies of the state. Nation-building efforts in the United States, as in other Western polities, were spurred by religious and economic leaders who held particular Protestant dictates as sacred: dislike for centralized authority, belief that the individual was the basic unit in the eyes of God, and faith that hard work and material transformation built character and spiritual virtue. These modest elites in eighteenth-century America were ministers, successful farmers, professionals, and municipal political leaders.

Their sacred commitments would be blended with a more hierarchical form of bureaucratic authority as corporate organization and mass production arose in the late nineteenth century. It was not simply coincidental that the bureaucratic factory became the magical model for recasting the one-room rural schoolhouse into a mass institution able to efficiently process more modern children. For this was the organizational form that awarded the school greater legitimacy in the eyes of economic and political elites. Over time, faith in the corporate form of mass schooling and its moral order has come to be institutionalized in the minds of political leaders—be they working in the central state or within local school districts spread throughout the United States.[23]

The younger, more fragile state, common across the Third World, plays a much stronger role in importing and legitimating the bureaucratic structure and moral order of the Western school. Bureaucratic administration signals "modern practice," particularly in societies where rationalized organizations or firms are still a novel form. Here the visible contours and symbols of "modern organization" take on enormous power. The Third World school may fail to hold deep effects on children's acquired literacy or secular values. But the fact that the school is tightly administered—with tidy accounts, a sharp schedule of classes, and attractive gardens—signals the attributes of a modern organization. The institution is recognized by local parents as a concrete instrument of modernity, even if the school's technical objective of raising children's literacy is rarely accomplished.[24]

Theory 3—World Institutions

North American scholars, emphasizing the worldwide similarity of states and schools, are exploring a third explanation for the expansion and deepening of mass schooling. This provocative intellectual movement, led by sociologist John W. Meyer, offers a social theory which parallels work on economic world-systems. World *institution* theorists point out that Western ideals and forms of organization, having oozed throughout Western consciousness, jump across national boundaries and root within emerging nation-states. This institutional movement spreads relentlessly, independent of a particular society's wealth, location relative to core European and North American economies, or variation in observable structure of the state. If functionalist or class theorists were correct, this cross-national variation in economic and state variables should explain differing levels of school enrollment. Meyer and colleagues attempt to show that they do not. Instead, they claim that mass schooling exercises an institutional life of its own, legitimated and reproduced within the Western state's logic which now transcends national boundaries.[25]

Earlier Marxist or *dependencia* theorists saw expansion of state and school as determined by the nation's relative status in the world economy. Fellow critical theorists also emphasize the role of ideology, class structure, and changing patterns of labor demand in explaining the expansion of mass schooling. Yet world institution theorists argue that the Western school, as an organization surrounded by popular support and symbols of modernity, spills over national boundaries regardless of these nation-specific factors. Mass schooling has expanded rapidly in almost all Third World countries since World War II. Despite scarce economic resources, political elites in poor states struggle to express their own legitimacy and signal modernity by building more and more Western-looking schools.

World institution theorists describe why mass schooling is such an attractive *political good*—whether we focus on post-Reformation Europe, contemporary First World nations facing instability, or fragile Third World states. As political and economic elites proceed with building a centralized state and legitimating bureaucratic forms of organizing, they risk alienating plural elements of the polity or local tribes which have not yet been incorporated. Here the legitimacy of the current government declines, and the long term institutionalization of the state apparatus slows. By unobtrusively nudging the expansion of mass schooling, the state (a) crisply illustrates how children can join the modern polity, (b) advances a meritocratic, not a tribal or particularistic, opportunity structure, and (c) mobilizes signals of modernity, from pushing high-status secular knowledge to rhetorically linking school attainment with access to wage-sector jobs.

Meyer and his colleagues are revitalizing Durkheim's (functionalist) fascination with symbolic action and ritual. Here the observable bureaucratic structure of state and school is secondary; more important are the *signals* that move between the state (or its agent, the teacher) and the individual child. Whether states and schools are centrally administered (say, in France) or locally controlled (as in the United States), signals about authority, "correct behavior," valued forms of achievement, and high-status forms of knowledge are quite similar across Western societies.

An education ministry's material resources or formal lines of administration are *not* the influential devices that shape local behavior and belief. What really holds the school organization together is whether teachers enact the bundle of beliefs and behavior that echo the state's agenda or which fit normative roles reproduced within the school itself. Teachers, for instance, are pushed to hold, as sacred, certain pedagogical practices and forms of knowledge: lecturing before pupils, exercising hierarchical authority, employing standardized tests, teaching "modern knowledge," be it teaching kids to speak French or teaching kids how to use computers. Administrative control of these disparate elements is problematic. In exacting conformity to these symbolic actions, however, the state and the teacher demonstrate their *shared faith* in the modern school's utility and the state's legitimate role in shaping the form and content of classroom action. As Meyer suggests, we should evaluate the school institution as a religious structure. Productive bureaucracies, like factories, possess singular goals, clear technical methods, and uniform elements for assembling a tangible good. None of these features characterize the production of literacy or achievement within the mass school organization.[26]

The Polity's Institutional Bedrock

Critical historians emphasize how European states, then the United States, have pushed to integrate other societies into the West's *economic* network: through mercantilist policies, outright colonial conquest, and more recently through development programs that export Western forms of market, firm, and state throughout the Third World. World institution theorists, however, back up and focus on the *institutional foundations* that serve to legitimate and culturally support Western economies. Third World states' desire to strengthen ties with the West, for instance, is driven by the perception that concrete economic benefits will result. But ongoing incorporation of societies into the West's economic network also is motivated by fragile states' simple desire to *look modern*—to build Western institutions, to mimic bureaucratic forms of organization, and to absorb secular language, knowledge, and meanings. To be seen as a *real* state, government leaders must do certain things: establish market-oriented trade rules and diplomatic links to the West, codify uniform laws, adopt a common language, and construct rationalized social services. Meyer emphasizes that both new nations and established nations (shaken by economic or political troubles) attempt to build or reinforce central institutions. Constructing institutions involves not only inventing organization charts and putting up new facilities. It also requires legitimating Western forms of authority, organization, and ways of signaling the individual citizen's membership in the modern polity, the wage economy.

These elements of institution-building are surprising similar across rich and poor nations. Most Western-looking states rely on mass schooling as the primary device for incorporating tribal peoples or subcultures into the formal polity. To become a "citizen" (member of the polity), the individual must attend school to learn the dominant language, the virtues of bureaucratic authority, and the wisdom of Western knowledge. Children who leave school or adults who remain illiterate are stigmatized as "unmodern" and categorized as being on the distant periphery of society.

The school, of course, may be impotent in accomplishing these objectives in a material way. But by simply extending the franchise, via the school, the state signals its own authority and its capacity to deliver access to modern forms of organization. By mimicking modernity, both new and old states seek to expand schooling and to strengthen the school's influence over children and their parents. Let's turn to a couple illustrations.

When the British were finally thrown out of Nyasaland in the early 1960s, Kamuzu Banda returned home to rule this new east African territory which came to be called Malawi. He was schooled in the United Kingdom and worked as a doctor in Scotland while in self-imposed exile. Banda returned with a deep affection for the British school structure. He quickly began building schools, training teachers in English and classical subjects, and requiring students to sit for the Cambridge exam. This west European system was layed on top of a society comprised of over thirty different tribal groups spread throughout a largely rural country, each ethnic group speaking its own language. One can now travel for two days off the (only) highway in Malawi and find a one-room hut with a teacher who instructs rural children in English (with a faintly British illiteration) about the history of modern Europe.[27]

Socialist Ethiopia provides a second example of how the state benefits from the importation of Western schooling. Since 1974 this highly centralized state has attempted to collectivize peasant farmers. Previously dispersed throughout the countryside in small family villages, the government coaxes peasants to move into larger communes by offering better water supplies, free primary schooling, adult literacy programs, and health care services. These communes, populated by one hundred to two hundred families, look like uniform suburban housing tracts, except that these tidy rows of shelters are huts glued together with red mud and thatch. In an effort to build "the socialist man," the government is rapidly expanding and rationalizing secular schools with support from a bizarre set of bedfellows. Each day advisors from East Germany, Holland, and the World Bank are discussing how to build schools faster or how to deepen the education ministry's administrative control over the local commune schools. Interestingly, the government's conception of schooling reflects a blend of Marx, Engels, and Dewey— encouraging children to work cooperatively, to value the integration of manual farmwork and intellectual activity, and to become loyal to the central state and party structure. Dislike for the West's preoccupation with individualism and exclusively mental work is clear within the government. But mobilization of the school institution and reliance on a (centralized) bureaucratic form is just as strong in eastern-bloc Ethiopia and in West-aligned Malawi.[28]

Wholesale borrowing of the Western school is best illustrated within, yet not unique to, the Third World. Francisco Ramirez and John Boli, for instance, describe how less wealthy, less unified European nations in the early nineteenth century began importing secular schools from higher-status European states as a strategy for becoming more competitive militarily and economically.[29] In contemporary times, political leaders within industrialized nations are eager to borrow the alleged discipline, toughness, and technical content of Japanese schooling—since their method of schooling must explain their economic success. Certain actions signaling "school improvement" become irresistible, including requiring kids to take more math courses, buying computers for classrooms, or pushing teachers to assign more homework. Whether such reforms actually boost pupil achievement or influence economic growth is not a question taken seriously by proponents. These initiatives are built on faith and hold sufficient symbolic value, signifying further movement toward "modern practice" and, incidentally, reinforcing the credibility of political elites.[30]

Why is the school such a seductive device for the Western state to employ? World institution theorists argue that political elites are motivated by romantic ideology, particularly a belief that the individual child can develop if purposefully socialized. This appealing faith invites individual membership in the polity and unifies faith in modern forms of child socialization. The latter purpose has long been articulated by Western philosophers of the state; the former point, the emphasis on membership, is originally highlighted by world institution theorists. The state constructs an individual entitlement to schooling. Since everyone is entitled, mass education must be expanded rapidly, and the schooling treatment must be administered uniformly. The state argues that it is dedicated to the *individual* child's development. But rapid and symbolic extension of franchise and membership is far more cost-effective for the state, especially for poor states, than any sustained concern with the child's actual development or achievement.[31]

The "individual" is reified under romantic Western ideology, cast as a creature with autonomy, developmental potential, and self-interested rationality. The notion of an individual, disembedded from local collectives, did not emerge with force until after the Reformation. The Western state would eventually borrow the Protestant tenet that the individual's link with God need not be mediated by an encumbered church structure. The individual could possess distinct characteristics and rights that were directly defined by the secular state. Local collectives—the family, church, village authorities, and firms—could not get between the state and its direct access to the individual. As Meyer and his colleagues persuasively argue, the Western state expressly attempts to stigmatize "traditional" local collectives. Joining and continued membership in the mass school become a powerful signal that the child is playing the state's game—pursuing secular socialization and preparing to enter the modern polity and the wage-economy.[32]

This process recasts the individual's fundamental institutional affiliations. Children in many east African tribes, for example, are raised by several adults in the village. Perceiving one's own child as somehow different or as an "individual" rarely occurs. The village collectively grows most necessary foodstuffs. Adults may walk to a market center once a week to trade their crops or chickens for a little meat, sugar, or a needed basket. The village headman or the mission church provides spiritual advice. Children attend the government primary school for three years on average, gaining a faint taste of European literacy, bureaucratic social rules, and modern symbols. This situation is not unlike what Durkheim found in the hinterlands of nineteenth-century France, or what contemporary inner-city teachers find in trying to touch disadvantaged youth. Most children will never participate in the core polity or succeed within the wage-economy. The state *is* successful in stigmatizing and eroding the status of local associations. But unless these kids can prove sufficient loyalty and achievement in terms of the school's knowledge and bureaucratic rules, they will not benefit from the opportunities so often promised by the state.

Empirical Evidence

The rise of competing theories, and heated debate among contentious adherents, has far outpaced progress on the more arduous task of empirical verification. Since the 1960s, many studies have seriously questioned the basic tenets of the functionalist-modernity line (drawing on historical data, local surveys, and contemporary ethnographic evidence). More recent empirical tests of class imposition models, however, also have shown mixed results. Evidence that undercuts universal claims made by world institution theorists also is emerging. Now that hard evidence is catching up with the more provocative exercise of theorizing, a clearer picture is coming into focus that highlights the parallel forces of country-specific conditions *and* ideological and economic imperatives which are exercised across all Western polities.

This section reviews major empirical findings that support or question the validity of each theory in explaining the *expansion* of mass schooling. More detailed reviews are available elsewhere.[33] Here I emphasize the practical importance of these empirical challenges, including implications for how we envision the growth of schooling and the meanings we attach to this robust phenomenon. Second, I show how empirical work is leading to more careful development of theory. The review below, for instance, leads us back to a conception of the fragile state that emphasizes country-specific conditions, particularly the state's capacity to manage its interdependencies within an uncertain institutional environment (as introduced in Chapter One). This avoids the danger of making universal claims—linked to one of the three grand theories—irrespective of the institutions and conditions which characterize a particular society or state. Evidence on the validity with which each theory explains the *deepening* of schooling is reviewed in Chapter Four.

Functional-Modernity: Shot Full of Empirical Holes?

Does mass schooling expand as a rational response to demands expressed by the state and the economy? The neo-classical liberal answer is an exuberant, "yes!" As national economies form and industrialization arises, new jobs emerge that require higher levels of literacy and technical skills. The liberal state, responsible for building basic infrastructure, rationally invests in universal schooling. Individuals benefiting from schooling prove to be more productive in the labor force and thus earn more. Parents, being rational optimizers, push their children to stay in school longer to gain better jobs in the modern economy. The accumulation of these local, individual decisions leads to aggregate growth in mass schooling, then to gains in national economic output. Empirical work focusing on this interaction between economic change and subsequent demand for more schooling is now voluminous.[34] Let me simply summarize major empirical findings that seriously challenge modernization theory.

Theoreticians' claims that economic gains drive school expansion, and that an economic calculus operating at the individual level motivates enrollment, have received inconsistent empirical support. Recently published historical evidence sharply challenges this degree of economic determinism as represented within modernization theory. First, secular mass schooling usually takes hold and enrollments shoot upward long *before* industrialization, even prior to the formation of commercial networks. Primary school enrollments, for example, in nineteenth-century France, England, and the United States were quite high (exceeding 30 percent of the child age group) decades before commercial integration and expansion. In addition, most Third World societies have witnessed explosive growth in mass schooling since World War II. Interestingly, empirical work shows that a nation's level of economic wealth is unrelated to enrollment growth at the primary school level, particularly since World War II.[35]

Second, early industrial expansion in many nations has historically retarded, not spurred, enrollment growth. This is particularly damning to functionalist interpretations—including both modernization and class imposition viewpoints—in that capital appears to be *competing* with the school and state for the attention and labor of youth. During early industrial eras, the opportunity cost of staying in school, and foregoing novel blue-collar wage levels, is simply too high. On the other hand, enrollments in rural areas or for girls often are higher when school attendance is synchronized with (seasonal) labor demands. Evidence of this negative relationship between early industrial growth and school enrollment has emerged recently from historical studies in the United States, England, France, and Mexico.[36]

Third, the earliest demands to expand basic schooling, expressed by political or cultural elites, focused on training religious leaders, military officers, and state bureaucrats. The preparation of commercial leaders, or pushing mass literacy to help rationalize economies on a national scale, came much later historically. By that time (the mid-nineteenth century in Europe and the United States), the institution of secular schooling was well established and based on these earlier forms of demand. Earlier rules and content of the school institution persist, despite changes in the nature of external demands. For instance, one can easily observe forms of academic curriculum, elite or colonial languages of instruction (in the Third World), even counter-normative forms of pedagogy that hold status within the school institution, but which may have little utility within the economy.

51

Fourth, technological change may contribute to early enrollment growth, as families and nations come to believe that more schooling is required to fill more complex jobs. Yet the leading historical study (from the United States) found that enrollment effects stemming from technological gains diminished once primary and secondary schooling became mass institutions (when enrollments moved past two thirds of the child cohort). Sociologists Richard Rubinson and John Ralph found that enrollments continued to rise independently of changes in technology and labor productivity. They argue that in early periods of industrial and technological change, the link between school credentials and job status is rational. That is, employers and the state, acting to boost the supply of schooling and to sanction higher school attainment, are behaving in a functional manner. Yet once higher school credentials come to hold substantial status, independent of their link to actual labor demand or requisite technical requirements, employers and the state can not block further school expansion (at least not within the decentralized United States political-economy). Thus the expansion of schooling continues relentlessly—whether functional in capitalist economic terms, or not.[37]

Two related points remain clear within the empirical literature: children of wealthier families benefit disproportionately as mass education expands, and wealthier states are better able to build more schools. But this recent research warns against a deterministic view that Western-like modernization will invariably lead to school expansion. Historical conditions are quite important in explaining why mass schooling is growing, or declining, within a particular country context. We must distinguish between early periods of nation-building and school expansion, versus later periods when both the state and the school gain legitimacy and social authority. Also, within a particular society, we should check to see whether the school institution was firmly established prior to the secular state's rise within a particular setting. Or did mass schooling become an imperative only after the modern (albeit fragile) state arose, as in post-colonial nations? Finally, the quality and characteristics of schools themselves must be examined. School buildings can go up and children can enroll at a rapid pace. But this simply holds symbolic value. Whether the school is functionally fitting economic demands and motivations depends upon the content and efficacy of what goes on inside classrooms. We will revisit and elaborate on these conditions and distinctions.

Class Imposition: Empirical Attack on Modernization Theory

Class imposition theorists, like their modernization adversaries, see the school as functionally fitting and serving the interests of economy and state. Yet this critical framework emphasizes how the expansion of schooling reinforces the authority, ideology, and economic resources of elite classes, not the pluralistic interests of diverse communities and less powerful classes. Empirical work by class imposition scholars, in some cases, has disconfirmed claims made by modernization theorists. Yet recent research also refutes key arguments put forward by class imposition theorists.

Two basic lines of argument have been mounted. First, upper class families and political elites advocate the expansion of schooling to push economic growth and to advance the institutional and cultural foundations underlying economic rationalization. The second, stronger line of attack on modernization theory denies that school expansion even yields intended economic effects. Schooling serves only to reproduce the class structure, and the advantageous position held by elites within that order. Schooling legitimates and reinforces language, ideals, and technical skills that have been assigned authority by elite groups. But this does not mean that schooling yields any skill improvements (for individuals) or productivity gains (for nations). Here too, the state plays a critical role in sanctioning the expansion of schooling for the purpose of class and cultural reproduction, independent of economic functionality. My brief review highlights theoretical developments in the class imposition field, particularly those that lead us back to my conception of the fragile state and the importance of country conditions.[38]

The first development concerns how states or politics define the *opportunity structure*. Class imposition implies resistance from local disenfranchised groups. Indeed, critical theorists have mounted historical and contemporary evidence on how working-class communities, and their children, at times resist mass schooling that is pushed by elites, who draw on the license provided by the central state. However, some critical theorists have come to recognize that, over time, groups originally disenfranchised come to participate in mass schooling, eventually internalizing the claims of elites that such participation will lead to greater opportunity. Outright resistance, as mentioned above, is too crude of a representation. This does not mean that *conflict* between dominant and subordinate classes dissolves. The issue centers on interrelated questions: When does class conflict arise (within state organizations or the school)? What is the process which unfolds? How is it resolved, and whose interests are served in its resolution?[39]

The distinction between early periods of nation-building versus later eras of institutional reinforcement is critical in working out this contradiction between short-run "resistance" to, versus long-run acceptance of, mass schooling. The issue arises in Third World communities where most peasant children drop out of school at a very young age, and where many urban children leave school to enter small-scale commercial or factory jobs.

Let me clarify the historical or situational conditions under which class conflict would intensify or recede. I agree with world institution theorists that popular support for mass schooling is widespread and deep. I have visited too many African classrooms that are jammed with 80 to 150 young children to believe that "resistance" to schooling is substantial.[40] Yet why do children drop out at such a young age?

Here economists make the useful distinction between a *preference* (or taste) for some commodity versus the capacity to express actual *demand*. Thus, the second point is that families assess the link between school attendance and *socially constructed* opportunities. For the peasant farmer who needs an extra hand in the fields, or hopes to marry off a daughter at the normal age of thirteen or fourteen, continued school attendance is not rational. The same logic applies to the working-class kid in North America who, within his or her apparent opportunity structure, comes to see high school graduation or university training as not very relevant. They may see further schooling as legitimate and functional for others, but the opportunity costs (economically and socially) are excessive for themselves.

From this viewpoint, how institutions within a nation construct opportunities plays a critical role in whether mass schooling expands. Many African societies are still comprised primarily of subsistence farming families. Here the likelihood of children successfully moving into the wage sector is very small; thus the perceived opportunity cost of staying in school is quite high. Preference for schooling translates more quickly into expressed demand in, say, east Asian societies where the modern opportunity structure has been expanding rapidly. This does not imply that the relative position and status of certain classes is changing. But the probability of incorporating previously disenfranchised groups is much greater. Resistance to simple participation in schooling and other nation-wide institutions will more likely diminish, again keeping in mind that membership and participation does not mean that these institutions have any effect on class position.

Class *imposition* implies downward pressure by elites who are sitting on top of political or economic institutions. But let's think about Third World settings where the modern wage sector may enfranchise only 15 to 30 percent of the adult population. Here political elites struggle to expand wage employment and enable youth to move into this select circle of jobs and social position. Modern institutions are *pulling* relatively few youths into the wage sector, leaving most youths to continue their pattern of subsistence agriculture or minimalist survival in urban slums. Elites are not necessarily "imposing" certain economic or social roles. They and their institutions are selectively pulling-in youths who hold particular skills, language, and membership rituals which conform to modern sector norms.[41]

The second development relevant to the assessment of class imposition theories concerns *state invention of class differences*. States historically have shaped the structure of opportunity within their societies. During early nation-building, for example, fragile states encourage growth in a variety of service jobs, including teachers, postal clerks, and rail workers. To the extent that these jobs require basic literacy, school attendance is encouraged. Research in Mexico, for instance, shows that the state's incremental penetration into rural towns, and related growth in white-collar jobs, spurred school enrollment during the first half of the twentieth century. Growth in industrial jobs actually depressed enrollments, consistent with the historical evidence from the First World.[42] In many Third World nations today, civil service jobs continue to dominate the wage sector. The state-sanctioned status of these white-collar occupations is very high relative to rural agricultural, non-wage earning, and even mid-level industrial jobs.

The state also can arrange the supply of schooling in ways that provide variable access to jobs and economic opportunities. The French state, for instance, long supported two different tracks of secondary schools. The high-status track historically trained elite French bureaucrats and military leaders. The low-status track turned out white-collar workers for the commercial sector. Places in high-status secondary schools were limited and strictly rationed by admission procedures.[43] Similarly, Third World states often allocate modest resources to a mediocre mass primary school system. Then, a relatively high-quality secondary school system is more amply supported which disproportionately serves children from elite families. In some cases, political action can push the state to minimize class-related features of school systems. The structure of schooling in the United States is much less differentiated (at least prior to secondary school), being based on integrationist ideals embedded in the common school.[44]

State actions—school construction, expenditures, and policy initiatives—do influence enrollment growth in some settings. For example, state actions at boosting the local supply of schooling, or reducing direct costs by eliminating school fees, have been found to spark enrollment increases. Such findings are now available from historical studies in the United States, France, Mexico, and east Asia.[45] Importantly, these discrete state initiatives can boost or depress enrollments independently of economic growth or labor demands.

Sharp ideological signals from the central state also can encourage enrollment growth long before the government apparatus holds sufficient capacity to finance more schools and more teachers. The post-revolutionary French state, for instance, advocated mass schooling and placed the financial burden on local communes well into the nineteenth century. Primary school enrollments rose to over 50 percent of the child cohort prior to the central state's assumption of administrative and financial jurisdiction. Similarly, Third World states' rhetorical push on families to enroll their children in school far outpaces actual government capacity to build more schools and hire more teachers.[46]

Another development relevant to class imposition theories concerns the question of whether *school expansion leads to economic change,* as alleged by modernization theorists. Even critical researchers *do* find nation-level economic gains from the spread of mass schooling. Yet again, country-specific conditions are quite important. Universal claims are no longer defensible empirically. First, opportunity structures and schooling must open up in ways that encourage more efficient production of goods and services. For instance, growth in service jobs, often linked to state activities, does not necessarily spur economic growth. Nor is economic change likely to flow from opportunity structures and forms of schooling that simply reproduce class differences or caste structures (in terms of elite language, knowledge, and customs). The "democratization" of school opportunities must be harmonized with the liberalization of capital and change in the labor structure.

Second, the quality of schooling plays a large role in determining economic returns to educational expansion. The spread of low-quality schooling yields a strong symbolic return and significant political capital, especially for the fragile state. However, no economic benefits should be expected. A minimal threshold of educational quality must be reached before economic returns, in terms of productivity in agriculture or the wage-sector, are observed.[47]

Third, the state may be effective in convincing parents to keep their children in school. But this may result in lower production in the short-run, as youths are drawn out of agricultural and industrial labor. Here the state is competing with subsistence families and formal capital for the labor power of children and youths.

When the link between schooling and economic growth appears to be disappointingly weak, pressure builds within the Western state to strengthen this coupling. Over time, entry to and advancement within the modern wage-sector becomes more directly linked to school credentials. Signals of membership and status within the modern economy, or within state institutions, are expressed in the currency of school attainment. Allocation of school-related opportunity, however, can swerve way out of line when sharp change occurs in the economic opportunity structure. Heavy investments in vocational training, at one time, appeared to be a better way of linking schooling to wage-earning blue-collar jobs. But planners failed to see that the state was doing far more to legitimate and assign high status to white-collar occupations, especially in the Third World where industrial capital is very constrained.

Finally, as the state and employers struggle to link schooling and economic or skill demands, action is rarely taken to reduce class-based inequities. The mean level of schooling may rise for all groups in a society. But as more people obtain a given credential, be it a college degree (in the United States) or a primary school certificate (in the Third World), its value deflates and the lower classes remain at a competitive disadvantage. The state may be effective in extending the franchise of mass schooling, independent of economic forces. Yet the state's capacity to reorder economic opportunities for disadvantaged groups depends upon change in the job structure, not only upon extending a symbolic franchise in the modern sector through school enrollment.

Early Evidence: The State and School as World Institutions?

World institution theorists have shaken earlier conceptions of how Western organizations—especially the state and the school—grow and elaborate organizationally. Dominant conceptions of the state emphasize its technical-material task of building national infrastructure, including its eager attempts to serve economic imperatives by boosting the supply of schooling. The institutional viewpoint, instead, highlights the state's implicit ideological influence *and* sees the school as a distinctly different organization deeply embedded in the Western polity.

Here state and school are viewed as parallel, often independent hosts of Western cultural commitments. Both are deeply institutionalized within the worldwide network of Western polities, providing fundamental signals of what a "modern polity" should look like. Rather than relying on horizontal (division of labor) or vertical (class) categories to understand social organization, institutional theorists emphasize the importance of shared and sacred commitments regarding how modern organization and modern socialization should appear to operate.[48]

Within nations, as we have seen, technical and policy actions by different institutions help explain the spread of mass schooling, including traditions and opportunity costs facing families, wealth, change in labor demand, action by the central state and local agents, and even activity by local churches. The empirical problem for world institution theorists, then, is to show that underlying this technical action is a deeper set of cultural and political commitments that are moving *across national boundaries* and historical conditions.

Initial empirical work focuses on school enrollment rates across large samples of nations, then associates enrollment gains with cross-national variation in country wealth, type of central state (capitalist or centralized), and status within the world economy or position within the earlier colonial system. Looking only at the post-World War II era, John Meyer and his colleagues found that earlier school enrollment levels were, not surprisingly, the strongest predictor of later enrollment levels. More interestingly, they also found that economic wealth and state structure did *not* help explain cross-national variation in mass school enrollment, after taking into account earlier enrollment levels.[49]

This leading research group, more recently, extended their historical data back into the nineteenth century. Their initial findings do show that enrollments have historically lagged behind in nations that were once peripheral colonies, especially within nations which were French colonies. In general, national levels of wealth and state structure still do not explain cross-national variation in school enrollment, net the influence of prior school enrollment. Meyer's inference is that mass schooling was firmly institutionalized very early on, and it spreads as a broad social movement independent of economic and political forces. Post-colonial nations that gained independence since World War II, such as in Africa and Asia, entered the Western network rather late in historical terms. But even in these cases, school enrollments have quickly caught up with European nations and with countries which gained independence in the early nineteenth century (Latin America).[50]

This early empirical work from the world institution camp looks at only aggregate, nation-level enrollment rates—a measure indicating simple extension of the school franchise. State agencies have commonly over-reported enrollment rates, especially in post-colonial nations. In addition, children's daily rates of school attendance and levels of school quality, especially among Third World nations, vary dramatically across nations. Indeed, even rough indicators of educational quality, such as expenditures per pupil, have been found to depend upon a nation's level of wealth and on the (politically determined) size of the education sector.[51] World institution scholars, admittedly, are focusing on mass schooling as a symbolic form of membership in the modern polity, not as a technical instrument that imparts variable levels of literacy and social norms. Yet the process of (school) institution-building, and the antecedent force of other organizations, involves more than simple enrollment as the dependent outcome.

Nor have world institution theorists distinguished between eras of early nation-building versus later periods when mass schooling is broadly legitimated within the polity. Forces influencing school expansion may differ greatly, and such differences are of critical importance in understanding school expansion within young, fragile states. During early periods of nation-building (or within turbulent polities), elites appear to play a much larger role in expanding or constricting the growth of mass education. The school institution itself may have much less legitimacy, or its basic purpose may be heavily questioned. The world institution school de-emphasizes the role of elites; indeed the issue of agency is not addressed. Mass schooling is seen as a deep social movement with a bullish life of its own.[52]

Finally, world institution theorists can not really address why contemporary enrollment rates remain low, and are even declining, in many Third World nations. Here the distinction between institutional preference for formal schooling, versus the family's capacity to express actual demand over time, is particularly helpful. Nor does the theoretical perspective allow for the reintroduction of institutional competition from non-Western organizations, such as rising enrollments in Islamic and other non-government schools where the fragile state's credibility is dissolving.

Summary: Muffling the Sound of Clashing Symbols

This growing body of empirical evidence does indicate that the state can influence a society's level of faith, and enrollments, in mass schooling. Yet the state's two environments—institutions on which it depends and institutions on which it acts—sharply condition the efficacy of political elites. Many fragile states depend exclusively, for example, on entrenched economic institutions for their resources and legitimacy. Here the state's realistic capacity to signal mass opportunity, liberal economic change, or expansion of the school franchise is quite constrained. Yet in other cases, the state may move aggressively to expand mass schooling and to reorder economic organization, as a way of looking like a modern state and as a means for broadening popular legitimacy.

In addition, world institution theorists remind us that the formal school pre-dates the secular state, and may independently act out Western ideals regarding individual development, social organization, and moral character. The fragile state commonly mobilizes all the symbols and material attributes of mass schooling. But the school itself carries certain traditions and organizational forms that are not easily manipulated. Political elites, resources permitting, can rapidly build more clay structures, call them "schools," and ship-out a young teacher to stand before the class of eager children. But states are continually baffled by the failure of budgetary, administrative, and symbolic efforts in deepening the school's actual effect on their children.

Political elites act much like a conductor who is anxiously trying to ideologically orchestrate the sounds made by mischievous musicians. The conductor convenes the orchestra, often inviting new members and socializing them to the basic rules. The task of working out dissonant notes, however, is more complex, more subtle. He can try material sanctions or incentives. Yet a sweeter, more harmonious sound is not likely accomplished through regulation. Instead the conductor must cajole the orchestra to adopt a common language, to see and feel what is sacred. Divisive sounds from the percussion section or from the wind instruments continue to shatter this cooperative harmony attempted by the conductor—spurring the conductor to attempt fresh, gentler attempts at integrating the pluralistic tastes of each musing musician.

In many Third World societies the state apparatus is still viewed as particularistic, a foreign organization that acts with limited legitimacy. The local school, located in the village or urban shantytown, may hold greater authority. But despite parents' respect for its signal of opportunity, they simply can not afford to keep their children in school, given economic and cultural opportunity costs. Political elites must struggle to broaden their own credibility *and* to lessen intervening (local) economic and cultural commitments that limit the school's attractiveness.

The empirical literature points us toward the *conditions* under which the state can move effectively on this two-pronged agenda. Here we return to the fragile state's four basic facets (put forward in Chapter One). First, the state must position itself relative to interdependencies within an uncertain, often treacherous environment. This positioning may manifest a strong or a weak position relative to the force of other institutions, be they economic, religious, or family organizations.

Second, political actors must act upon lateral interdependencies for resources and upon downward interdependencies to incorporate local groups. Since the school may hold greater local credibility than the centralized state, the latter must respectfully pursue its rocky romance with the former. Often times, the state gains authority through its association with, and subsequent takeover of, local schools.

Third, the fragile state is energized, not by its functional harmony with static interests, but by fluid conflict between Western ideals and pre-modern (even indigenous) forms of authority, production, and socialization. Pressures to integrate trade and rationalize production, for instance, place the state in the role of building social and physical infrastructure. But this runs headlong into strong economic interests, often uncovering government elites among the stakeholders. Village leadership also looks askance at the central state's relentless efforts to penetrate the hinterlands and undercut traditional collectives and forms of authority. The state both frames these conflicts, then attempts to cool the hot ideological and material contests that emerge. This places the state in the pivotal position of the mediator with unquestioned legitimacy.

Fourth, the state's own capacity to exert influence depends upon its internal administrative, technical, and symbolic capacities. It must find effective methods for managing its interdependencies and controlling its own agencies. As a fragile organizational apparatus, the state must develop its own internal workings. Otherwise its already brittle capacity to protect its own institutional boundaries and turf will shatter, and its ability to penetrate the geographical and civic hinterlands will erode.

We next turn to these levers and workings located within the state—the symbolic and organizational devices that political actors manipulate as they struggle to grow more modern children.

3

Winding Up Schools: The State Constructs Teachers' Roles and Tools

On the edge of Blantyre, the commercial center of Malawi, I was visiting a relatively well endowed primary school. Situated in rolling, sparsely wooded hills, students were benefiting from energetic teachers and ample numbers of textbooks. As I walked into the headmaster's office, that piercing brightness of the southern African sun bounced off his recently white-washed walls.

Bookshelves rested against one wall—holding only wafer-thin booklets. The luminescent white wall laying behind the shelves and these flat booklets was entirely visible. As it turned out, each of the school's forty-five teachers had one of these booklets to sign in and out of work each day—a simple pencil-and-paper timeclock! Consistent with the clean walls and tidy method of supervision, this headmaster had a neat schedule of classes posted on an otherwise bare bulletin board. He promptly pulled out his ledger showing which families had paid required school fees, so elegantly recorded it would put to shame any self-respecting American accountant. The headmaster seemed unconcerned that he had no books, just administrative artifacts. I asked how often he would visit each teacher's class to assess instruction. He tightened his brow, trying to attach some meaning to the question's secondary clause, and responded: "Oh, sir, about once a year."

My colleague was observing a classroom in another school. Presenting an English lesson, the teacher was marching through the script laid out within the national textbook. Earnest curriculum writers had included "questions to encourage discussion" at the back of this particular chapter. But African teachers in former British colonies rarely ask pupils questions, except perhaps to recall simple bits of information. So, this teacher simply had the pupils shout out these "questions" in unison. The teacher did not recognize that these were queries to be debated, rather than additional material simply to be recited.[1]

Sculpting Teachers' Roles and Tools

State actors constantly try to animate the school and shape the action of its local residents—principals, teachers, and students. Political actors at central and local levels eagerly attempt to wind up the school and aim it in a particular direction. Often, however, the school organization careens out of control. Earnest attempts at bureaucratic control often yield unexpected results, as seen in southern Africa.

Education ministries throughout the world recurrently intervene with discrete programs or administrative reforms. Yet these "modern forms of management," for instance specifying a curricular script for teachers to follow, often yield results that have no effect on pupils' achievement. At times education offices, acting as agents of fragile centralized states, *do* efficaciously guide the behavior of local school residents. But the result of "tight management," as seen above in Malawi, can be headmasters who act as petite bureaucrats, not as school-level leaders motivating instructional improvement. Or it can result in teachers, thoroughly socialized to follow the standard routinized lesson, who befuddle enlighted curriculum writers that earnestly try to encourage more stimulating interaction between teacher and pupil.

At other times, state interventions are simply lost, disappearing down that dark organizational hole—the local school. Should we even visualize the school as an *organization*? The local school rarely resembles a coherent institution comprised of *interdependent* actors. The teacher's work is performed in isolation from other adults. He or she holds enormous discretion over whether certain instructional tools or state-sponsored interventions are mobilized, or quietly laid to rest.

To be felt at the school level, state actors often move to reduce the work of headmasters and teachers into discrete, predictable tasks. The paradox that arises is that the wrong tasks often are rationalized and sanctioned. We see this with headmasters who spend hours keeping their accounts straight, yet never visit classrooms to coach teachers. Similarly, routinization of the teacher's work squeezes out even slight complexities that may be critical to learning, such as addressing children's questions or checking to see if pupils are comprehending the lesson. Fragile, centralized states rarely have the resources to actually regulate the prescribed behavior expected of headmasters or teachers. When state actors are administratively effective, symbols of "modern management" or "proper teaching" often are monitored, not actions which boost the quality of pedagogy or the performance of pupils.

Practical Dilemmas Facing the State

This chapter moves us toward the local school, describing how, and with what effect, *state actors attempt to shape the teacher's role and behavior in the classroom and to mold tools made available to the teacher.* In short, the state eagerly attempts to sculpt the social rules enacted by the teacher *and* the instructional technology employed to reinforce curricular content (overt or hidden). This chapter explores the territory that stretches from the state's motivations to concrete actions undertaken by state actors aimed at shaping life in classrooms. Chapter 4 will complete this progression, reporting on how teachers, working under fragile states, enact their role and employ (scarce) instructional materials within their classrooms.

We have reviewed the forceful ideological and economic *imperatives* that push the fragile state to expand mass schooling and to signal mass opportunity. All Western states also must push to deepen the school's effects. Yet action on these imperatives bounces back at state actors with *nagging contradictions.* The conflict in ideals that most bewilders the state is that of the pursuit of mass opportunity set against a romantic commitment to individual development. The corporate state and mass schooling can effectively nurture within individual youths an atomistic capacity to act and achieve within markets and bureaucracy. But elements of the Western polity keep pushing for a broader conception of human capacity and growth.

Here, let's focus on four concrete ways in which the state attempts to shape the teacher's roles and tools within the classroom. These highly-charged fronts spring from political imperatives embedded within the Western state and operate as popularized expectations of the political elites. But fragile states—poor in material resources, technical know-how, and social authority—confront practical dilemmas as they move on these fronts.

These four areas of state intervention *do* influence the teacher's role in the classroom and the tools made available, although these effects often are inadvertent. As the state moves on each strategy, political actors and education bureaucrats quickly confront dilemmas and contradictions. After outlining these political imperatives, I describe how each imperative, and its paradoxical backside, is played out within the fragile state of Malawi.

- The fragile state continues to *rapidly expand mass education*, portraying new schools as the arrival of mass opportunity and modern progress. But material resources and technical know-how are so scarce that educational quality erodes relentlessly. The state and international agencies, earnestly committed to expanding mass schooling and to lending Western capital, encourage greater dependency and higher levels of debt. The state's fiscal capacity is stretched both by forceful popular demands to broaden opportunity and by rising dependence upon Western resources and institutional forms.

- Mass opportunity is signaled, but actual growth in the modern wage-sector is very slow. Thus *the educational system above primary school remains highly selective* with disproportionately high subsidies going to affluent families who can afford the opportunity costs of keeping their children in school through secondary and university levels. Government schools gain greater legitimacy in urban areas but remain a foreign institution (of the particularistic state) within the hinterlands. A national examination scheme attempts to represent a fair process for selection and mobility, but does little to help schools boost children's achievement or lessen class inequality. The state may inventively attempt to recognize cultural diversity in rural areas and to more effectively incorporate these peripheral children, that is, extend membership in the secular school.

- *Status, pay, and working conditions for teachers erode* as demands to expand enrollments outpace the state's fiscal capacity. The teaching occupation—*the* original job in the wage-sector after independence for literate Africans—becomes undesirable relative to private-sector employment. Important class differences emerge even within the small wage-sector.

- The fragile state—traditionally strong in authority and weak in actual penetration of social spheres—tries to order secular socialization *and* look modern by *routinizing the bureaucratic management* of local schools. Mechanical standardization of school management, pedagogical practices, and curricula, signals crisper state control and the reduction of organizational uncertainty. Modern management and teaching practices signal greater concern with educational quality and deepening of the school's effects on children.

Targets and Methods of State Action

When state actors—especially those in education ministries—act from these social imperatives they do not always take precise aim at controlling the teacher's role and classroom tools. Yet teachers often feel the rather blunt interventions undertaken by political actors. For instance, the fragile state's eagerness to rapidly expand school enrollments in the absence of sufficient resources has led to skyrocketing class sizes across the Third World. This forces the teacher to routinize instruction and focus on maintaining control, greatly altering the teacher's basic role and behavior in the classroom.

Education ministries (or local education offices) are most concerned with ensuring that schools simply are operating. *Organizational maintenance* takes up the bulk of administrators' time, not the *technical task of boosting student achievement*. This is frequently true of schools in the United States and other industrialized countries.[2] And state actors' concern with organizational maintenance is even greater in the Third World, where uncertainties are rampant: teacher salaries often arrive weeks late, textbooks are lost within the distribution process, headmasters frequently hop on the bus to town in search of teacher salaries and basic materials.

State actors draw upon three methods as they attempt to influence either the maintenance of schools or the technical task of boosting pupil achievement. First, governments "decide" on levels of support for the education-sector and allocate available resources to various inputs. Given the social welfare and employment function of schools, fragile states appropriate the bulk of support in the form of teacher salaries.

Second, state actors establish administrative forms or social rules that hold the school "system" together. Fragile states, building from colonial forms of administration, tend to be centralized and rely on classic, hierarchical social relations. When educational reforms are attempted, they are embedded in this traditional bureaucratic structure. So, changes are translated into a Weberian sequence of reducing complex tasks into routinized steps which are then sanctioned through hierarchical regulation. Universal and standardized solutions—salary schedules, curricula, and teacher behavior—are viewed as optimal under this vision of "modern administration."

Third, education ministries attempt to control the content of what is taught in the classroom. This involves shaping several tools—a universal curriculum, standard materials, teacher guides, and national examinations that enforce routinized forms of knowledge and "facts." In much of the Third World, standardized syllabi and curricula encourage pupils to memorize a variety of facts and knowledge-bits that are regurgitated when the pupil sits for the national exam. (Following the Third World, this pattern is becoming more legitimate in the United States.) Educational tools invented by the state often reinforce the social rules and form of classroom management enacted by the teacher. Throughout Africa, for example, lessons involve frequent oral recitation of vocabulary or arithmetic exercises, delivered in unison by all pupils. This mechanical process, set by the curricula or teacher guide, helps control and engage the fifty to ninety restless pupils that commonly sit before the teacher. Thus curricular content helps signal and legitimate certain forms of authority and human interaction that come to be seen as normal in a modern (hierarchical) organization.

This third method of influence by state actors also operates far above the classroom, unfolding at an institutional level. Third World newspapers frequently report the chief of state's admonition to parents that they must enroll their child in school, and encourage dedication to the child's studies. The state associates simple membership in the school organization with desirable moral or sacred qualities: nudging the child to work hard, accept modern forms of knowledge and belief, and achieve within the formal system of socialization and job preparation. The school is used as a stage upon which political elites enact ideologies and symbols which they hold as sacred, and which enhance the process of nation-building and reinforcing modern ways of growing up.

Figure 3.1 illustrates how the state's two *targets* of influence match its three *methods* of influence. State agencies and actors can allocate resources that aim to simply maintain the school institution, putting out money for teacher salaries, building maintenance, or textbooks (box 1).

Figure 3.1 The State's Targets and Methods of Influence

Targets

Methods	Organizational Maintenance and Membership	Technical Efforts to Raise Pupil Achievement
Resource allocations	1 —teacher salaries —facilities	2 —inputs linked directly to pupil literacy gains
Regulation of social rules	3 —sanctioning pupil attendance reporting by headmasters —requiring teacher lesson plans	4 —illustrating or encouraging effective teaching practices
Legitimization of knowledge and symbols	5 —writing textbooks that contain basic knowledge in the official national language	6 —enforcing teacher presentation of facts & knowledge forms that appear on the national exam

Sometimes the state may even think carefully about what physical inputs, ways of organizing, or pedagogical improvements could effectively boost pupils' levels of achievement (boxes 2 and 4). State actors can also engage in symbolic action, absent any new resources or administrative tightening, for example, encouraging teachers to set higher achievement standards (boxes 5 and 6).

Poor States: Scarce Material and Social Capital

State actors must spend material and social capital in their attempts at shaping the roles and tools of teachers. These two forms of capital comprise the currency through which states attempt to influence local schools. Fragile Third World states are usually poor in material resources. Even established European or North American states may be stingy when it comes to financing education. And all states suffer recurrent crises in political legitimacy. Thus scarcities of both material and social capital commonly arise. State actors and local activists often talk about the risk of burning too much political capital, that is, advocating policy change that is unpopular and undercuts the credibility of a government or particular politician. This often arises when central state actors attempt to push reforms on local schools that challenge the authority of local teachers or community leaders.

The term "social capital," advanced by sociologist James S. Coleman, encompasses a broader set of social rules.[3] First, remember that the state (even in established Western polities) remains as one particularistic actor surrounded by a variety of institutions and ideological currents. Second, state actors constantly attempt to reinforce the legitimacy of their agenda and their agencies, forming interdependencies with other organizations from which resources are gained and upon which the state's interests can be enacted. From this interplay, a variety of obligations or *social contracts* arise, implicitly limiting the state's legitimate role and methods of influence. Other organizations and members of the formal polity come to hold certain *expectations* about what state actors can and can not do. The state, over time, runs into these constructed boundaries of legitimate activity. Pushing these boundaries back or moving them significantly requires expenditure of considerable political points, or more broadly, social capital.

How is social capital accumulated and where does it reside within state institutions? Coleman defines social capital by its function. That is, it productively allows two or more actors (individuals or organizations) to pursue an objective that would be impossible to attain in the absence of expectations, trust, or implicit obligations that limit their interdependent action. Social capital itself lies in the structure or sinew that exists between two actors. No explicit exchange occurs between the two actors, as market definitions of cooperation would have it. Instead the norms and expectations of interdependence binding the two implies that both parties will benefit in the long run far beyond a single transaction and beyond economic rewards.

The state, for example, has historically argued that schooling provides young people an entry into the modern wage-sector and a higher-status way of life. In the Third World, the learning of European languages in school has long signaled that this modern school organization is carrying one's children into the promised land of a steady wage and richer culture. When the fragile state attempts to shift the language of instruction to an indigenous tongue, popular resistance is often swift and strong. The fledgling middle class *expects* that the school and the state are transforming their children, not reinforcing traditional ways. By pushing this progressive change, local people see the state as violating its institutional *obligation*. The central state must expend a good deal of social capital and trust to effectively implement a change in language policy.

The state can *build and accumulate* social capital if it shrewdly taps pockets of resources and symbols that circle about it. Once, while I was on a "mission" to Mexico City for the World Bank, headlines appeared in daily newspapers claiming that our efforts aimed to cut government spending for social services, then suck up the saved revenue to help repay the nation's foreign debt. (There was a large grain of truth in the government's well timed attack.) This manipulation of nationalistic fervor is a common device for adding to the state's stock of social capital. Within the education sector, state actors often link school expansion or quality gains to economic growth. Here, political elites draw on sacred Western beliefs or faith that the school contributes to individual development which, in turn, spurs economic expansion. Dipping into the symbolic scriptures of materialist secularism, the state projects its obligations, commitments, and builds *a trust with the polity* that it can deliver.

The State Surrounds Contested Terrain

The state, energized by the institutional imperatives that spark its action and limit its legitimacy, attempts to shape the school, particularly the teacher's role and tools. Political elites can, over time, encircle the school institution, even intensify strategies for maintaining and expanding it. Yet the nagging contradictions facing the state, as well as recurrent scarcities of material and social capital, constrain the fragile state's capacity to control the school. The local school organization is a contested terrain that the state attempts to surround and influence.[4] But this organizational landscape is slippery for state actors. Planting a flag that remains standing over time remains quite difficult.

Shortly I turn to the case of Malawi, illustrating the difficulties faced by a fragile state as it moves on the four political-educational imperatives introduced above. We will see that as the state creeps up on the school, often rather loudly, these nagging contradictions and shortages of capital dampen actual levels of control which political actors can achieve.

Where's the Glue? Pasting the School Together

Many state actors view the school as a classic bureaucracy. Sure, it suffers from inefficiencies and "poor management." But the school's effects on children can be deepened through conventional Weberian remedies: tighter hierarchical control of school staff and students; reduction of complex work (teaching) into prescribed and routinized tasks; development of more specialized roles; and standardization of knowledge into bits and pieces that can be more easily tested. This conventional push to "rationalize" school management is relentless under fragile states, where political actors must signal an interest in deepening the school's effects. Bureaucratic progressives surface even within decentralized states, such as the United States, when political institutions are faced with economic competition from outside or with moral instability from within. Clamping down on the school signals political commitment to improving the socialization of youth, independent of what effects are felt within the classroom.

Critics of this school-as-factory conception point out that such mechanized medicines can be counter productive. Teachers resist the deskilling and de-professionalization of their work. The learning process, increasingly controlled from above through extrinsic sanctions, also may become less motivating to children, especially as the morale and intrinsic commitment of their teachers decline.[5]

Others argue that bureaucratic reforms are bound to fail since they are built upon a misunderstanding of what cements the school organization together. These critics, coming from an institutionalist viewpoint, argue that the school is a loosely coupled set of teachers who are herded about, but not really controlled by, local administrators. What teachers actually do in the classroom has been ritualized and institutionalized: lecturing at children, following the school's official knowledge (that may be disconnected from the outside world), giving exercises or dittos, and evaluating children's retention in mechanized ways.

State actors or local school principals may attempt to change the behavior of teachers. But the teacher often remains autonomous within his or her classroom, inventively buffering external pressures.[6] Institutional theorists point out that local school authorities do create programs and hire specialized staff, often in response to categorical interventions pushed by central state agencies. This administrative adaptation to external demands may simply buffer the state's attempt to penetrate into the classroom. Local school authorities may symbolically meet the legal and regulatory requirements of a particular reform, yet accomplish little change in teachers' behavior and beliefs. At times, categorical school programs actually encourage more atomistic, isolated action by teachers. School regulators attempt to change the individual teacher's behavior, for example, within school programs for disadvantaged children. But these controls often distract from efforts to boost the teacher's professional discretion and cooperative action with other school staff.[7]

Institutional theorists usefully see the school as a bounded organization that holds similar contours and content across quite different societies and states. The school is held together largely by the *ritualized scripts* followed by headmasters and teachers—patterns of belief and behavior that are deeply ingrained within the institution. Indeed many teacher behaviors, whether reciting questions in Malawian classrooms or relying on dittos within United States classrooms, appear to be rather mindless—beyond simply occupying pupils and maintaining order.

Selective Coupling of State and School

The institutionalist conception of the school does beg three important questions. First, ritualized teacher behaviors reinforce a clear structure of authority, dominant social rules, and legitimate knowledge. In most southern African classrooms, students must stand when responding to the teacher's (often rare) question. If a "wrong answer" is given, the child must remain standing—up to 10 or 15 minutes. Or, around the world, we see that teacher pedagogy is moving toward the memorization of discrete bits of knowledge or facts (especially under "progressive" reform programs). This may not motivate children. But this ritual does signal that the teacher is an expert, the student's experience or opinion is unimportant, and the polity's press for universal knowledge and cultural forms is legitimate. Rituals employed to reinforce this agenda, including choral recitation in the Third World or multiple choice exams in the United States, are culturally arbitrary (to borrow Pierre Bourdieu and Jean-Claude Passeron's point). But these teacher behaviors do reinforce concrete social rules advocated by political elites.[8]

Second, state actors do occasionally penetrate the school's organizational boundaries—altering its social rules, knowledge embedded in these patterns, and teachers' own scripts and rituals. Within fragile

73

states, the drive to deepen the school's effect on children energizes various efforts to modify teachers' roles and tools. During periods of uncertainty within *established states* political elites often attempt to alter the authority of local school principals, confine the knowledge presented by, and behavior of, teachers, and fiddle with how special groups are treated in the classroom (ethnic minorities, the poor, the disabled). In parts of Africa similar efforts are being made to lessen the central authority of education ministries or provincial bureaucracies—instead giving school headmasters more discretionary resources and encouragement to improve instructional practices, rather than simply keeping tidy accounts.[9]

Third, institutional theorists fail to see that pressure from the state and dissent within the school itself prompt questions about teachers' rituals and scripts, as well as about how the bureaucratic organization of schooling reinforces these patterns within the classroom. Some teacher rituals are more sacred than others. The teacher must maintain order and encourage pupils to indicate their membership in, even loyalty to, classroom processes. But looking across societies or across time, the rules followed to weave this tight social fabric can vary. In Africa, several in-service training programs are trying to move teachers away from the common script of lecture-drill-recitation. Over the past two decades in the United States, teachers have tried various types of reading groups, "individualized instruction," cooperative learning strategies, and self-directed and regimented classwide lessons. The basic point here is that teachers and principals do at times reflect on what they are doing, questioning ritualized behaviors and associated effects on student motivation and achievement. Institutional theorists' disregard for individual agency and related shifts in teacher belief and behavior—as well as their disregard for the antecedent conflicts that prompt innovation—undercuts their position.

I prefer to see the school as a *selectively coupled* organization. That is, actors within the school institution, and those working between the state and school, may form interdependencies or hierarchical relationships along certain lines of activity. In Malawi, for instance, we will see that the national primary school curriculum is standardized and largely implemented within classrooms for the three subjects for which textbooks are available. Even relatively weak central states, such as the United States political structure, can tighten up or couple prescribed activities. Federal special education legislation, for example, requires certain uniform processes in how local schools and teachers handle disabled children. In many other domains, the loose-coupling image of North American schools is valid. Yet efforts in highly varied nation-states to standardize national examinations, reduce the complexity of knowledge contained in the curriculum, or homogenize teaching practices, represent efforts to selectively couple or manage vertical relationships between state and school.[10]

I concur with institutional theorists that the school's official administrative structure is of secondary importance. The glue holding together the school organization is made up of deep expectations and scripts that guide what teachers are supposed to do within the classroom. Importantly, these norms and rituals differ significantly across national, even regional, settings. Action by the state is one factor that may explain this variation, beyond the heritage defined by earlier cultural norms or colonial regimes (for instance, British versus French forms of authority and pedagogy in African schools). And although rituals and institutionalized behavior are slow to change, nothing is sacred in Third World nations that are bent on "modern change." Some state actors are questioning the stifling forms of teaching so common in African schools. Yet moves to alter the rituals of teachers may be swamped by the fragile state's preoccupation with expanding enrollments. Yet the state may selectively couple with elements of the school or teachers to shake the scripts upon which most teachers rely.

Keeping in mind these complexities about the school organization, we now turn to the four political imperatives which require state actors to nudge, cajole, even push the residents inside local schools. Fragile states must confront these imperatives, despite their recurring shortages of material resources and political legitimacy. The imperatives, grounded in the character of the Western state, can not be avoided. But they present hazardous dilemmas and contradictions. State strategies aimed at cooling out these contradictions and underlying social conflicts vary greatly across nations. Here we focus on how the Malawian state attempts to ease these tensions.

Imperative 1: Signaling Mass Opportunity

Just three institutions are present in most commercial towns of Africa: an open-air marketplace, a church mission, and a primary school. Building more schools—as rapidly as possible and regardless of quality—is a basic act of institution-building undertaken by the state. The brick-by-brick construction of a modest schoolhouse in a rural village or urban neighborhood is a sight to behold. The event turns out heads of state, tribal chiefs, and local functionaries.

Educational opportunity has risen dramatically since the independent state of Malawi was created in 1963. Initially this newborn state focused on expanding secondary education and technical training, a priority originally backed by the World Bank, arguing that anticipated industrial development required more skilled manpower. Yet, since the 1970s government policies have emphasized growth of primary school enrollments. The number of children enrolled has shot upward at 6.3 percent annually over the past two decades, far exceeding growth in child population. Primary school enrollments stood at 1.2 million in 1989. Secondary school enrollments have quintupled since 1963. The absolute number of pupils, however, equalled just 27,000 in 1989 (representing just 2 percent of primary school enrollments).[11]

Popular demand for, and institutional supply of, schooling had grown dramatically *prior to* creation of the Malawian state. Scottish missionaries opened the first recorded school in 1881, enrolling just two children. As early as 1927, the British administration in Malawi (then called Nyasaland) counted just under 3,000 schools. These modest institutions usually had just one teacher and operated within mission stations spread throughout small villages and trading centers. In 1924, for example, Catholic missions operated 571 village schools and claimed to enroll 27,000 children. Missions operated by the Church of Scotland enrolled about 15,000 pupils at this time. In 1927, the colonial administration created a department of education which provided small grants to mission schools.

Poverty and Class Differences

This case of early institution-building is remarkable, given the low level of economic and organizational development found even in contemporary Malawi. Let's focus on this context within which the state attempts to signal mass opportunity and modern change. Malawi is among the top ten poorest countries in the world. Annual income per capita entering the 1990s equaled just $160. The economy is founded upon the production, distribution, and export of raw commodities: tobacco, tea, ground nuts, and some sugar cane. Most Malawians participate only marginally in the cash economy. The vast majority of adults and youths still engage in subsistence agriculture, producing only a small surplus that can be taken to market.

Cash income is very low in Malawi. The average rural household earns the equivalent of $80 per year in the market economy. The average annual wage in the private sector, which employs 80 percent of all wage earners, equalled less than $400 in 1986. Government earnings run about 20 percent higher on average. Teachers earn about $800 per year.[12]

Malawi is comprised of over twenty-five distinct language groups. Chichewa is the official language as set by the state. This language is spoken by no more than half the population. It *is* the language spoken by political leaders and bureaucrats. The basic infrastructure that normally integrates nation-states is rudimentary in Malawi. One tarmack road spans the length of the country. There are two, yes two, traffic lights in the entire country. With limited communication networks—only 17% of all households have a working radio—modern knowledge and values are limited to a few towns. The most recent household survey (1984) revealed that only 14 percent of all Malawian women reported being aware of *any* form of birth control, including abstinence, child spacing, and modern contraceptives.[13]

Fifty percent of the population (over age 5) has *never* attended primary school. "Literacy" is poorly defined and badly measured; the rate among adults stands at about 15 to 20 percent. There is almost nothing to read in rural villages and trading posts. Only 15 percent of Malawi's 8 million people live in one of the nation's four towns. Life expectancy at birth is just 46 years, due largely to the fact that one fifth of all babies die before reaching age 1. Malawi's population, now growing at a rate of over 3.5 percent per year, will almost triple over the next 30 years.[14]

The state must rely on *signaling* mass opportunity, since the actual chance of a young Malawian entering wage employment is declining. Eighty-five percent of all Malawian adults remain engaged in agricultural production, a proportion which has not changed since the mid-1970s. Service employment, particularly within government, dominates the remaining share of the labor force. Government employment is growing at less than the rate of economic growth. Domestic production (GDP) has expanded at just 2.5 percent annually since 1980. Thus, a young Malawian's probability of entering wage employment—already just one in seven—is declining at the rate of 1 percent per year.

Distinctions among social classes are sharp within Malawi. Peasant farmers, as described above, still dominate the society in their numbers. Yet government elites and managers linked to parastatal firms dominate the political structure. Separating economic and political leaders is difficult, since government often controls lucrative commercial firms, including agricultural marketing and food processing concerns. The state, for instance, holds controlling interest in the company that prints school textbooks, revenues for which largely come from the World Bank. Between rural peasants and urban managers lie two groups: mid-level civil servants and shopkeepers, the latter group dominated by east Indians.

In 1968, one analyst estimated that the richest 10 percent of all Malawians gained 46 percent of the nation's annual wealth. The wealthiest 5 percent gained 39 percent of national income. By 1985, the class structure had become even less equitable. The richest 10 percent now benefited from 52 percent of national income. The share going to the poorest 60 percent of the population: just 19 percent of the national income.[15] Malawi's economy has demonstrated a capacity to grow, especially in the export of raw commodities. Yet this growth has served to reinforce class inequities rather than create fair incentives across broad segments of the population.

Scarcity of real opportunity, however, does not detract from the *illusion* of opportunity. If anything, signaling the chance to get ahead (materially) may be easier under such stark economic and social conditions. Yet the state faces economic constraints as it relentlessly builds schools and classrooms. The state faces two big uncertainties: the weather and international prices for export commodities. Since 1975, Malawi has suffered from three protracted periods of drought. Agricultural production grew at just 0.5 percent annually over the 1980s. Aggregate GNP rose at an annual rate of only 0.7 percent, way below population growth. Income on a per capita basis fell almost 3 percent each year over this dismal decade.[16]

One growth industry does show a great robustness in Malawi: the burgeoning level of debt owed to foreign lenders. The state's spending on debt service has jumped upward at 7.3 percent per year since 1980. Government now sends fully 38 percent of its recurrent budget to Western banks each year! All other recurrent spending rose at just 1.2 percent in real terms. State support to education grew at half this rate. The expansion of school enrollments slowed over the 1980s, perhaps due to intensifying economic pressures within urban and rural communities.

Primary school enrollments, nevertheless, are growing at 3.2 percent per year. Thus per pupil spending has *fallen*—2.6 percent annually since 1980. Thousands of more children are entering classrooms. But the state is unable to hire additional teachers, print necessary textbooks, or import sufficient supplies of paper on which pupils can write.

Take the case of Mkata Primary School, located on the outskirts of the capital city of Lilongwe. The headmaster reported an enrollment of 7,000 children! Over 1,600 children attend Standard 1 classes on an average day. So the school's sixteen Standard 1 teachers each face about one hundred children. This is not atypical of urban schools. The nation-wide ratio of pupils per teacher shot upward from 41:1 in 1970 to 67:1 by the end of the 1980s. At Nkata Primary, one third of all classes are taught outside, where the teacher stands with his or her blackboard in hand. The school has only twelve classrooms. So clusters of children, each numbering 50 to 120, appear across the grounds sitting on the beaten-down, red-clay ground, beneath sparse trees that buffer the Afri-can sun's penetrating intensity. The headmaster's most pressing prob-lems: overflowing latrines, lack of classrooms and desks (the school has just 150), and a severe shortage of paper.

Only 40 percent of all school-age children are enrolled in primary school nationwide. Of these, only one in five will finish the eight-year primary school cycle. The government estimates that one language textbook is available for every four pupils. One in three children receive an arithmetic text. Due to the state's fiscal constraints, spending per pupil has fallen dramatically, from $14 per pupil in 1980 to about $10 by the decade's end. This decline is manifest in the declining real earnings of teachers.[17]

Tasting Opportunity, Grasping at Symbols

Popular demand for mass schooling does slow when economic shocks momentarily require children to stay close to home—tending the garden and younger siblings, or working the streets to eke out a bit more cash. But even within materially poor societies like Malawi, the sweet aroma of possible opportunity kindles strong popular demand for schooling. African states try to keep out-front of this resilient clamor for mass education, given the rich symbolic rewards accruing to the state as it builds more classrooms and hires more teachers. Even as the actual odds of entering the wage-sector are declining, the illusion of opportunity becomes bigger and brighter as more children are crammed into decrepit classrooms.

The fragile state thus comes to rely on *signaling* mass opportunity. Even this strategy is not cheap for resource-poor states. As in Malawi, government budgets can not keep pace with the collective hunger for a wage-earning job and membership in the high-status, modern polity. However, more serious efforts to shake the class structure—distributing wealth more fairly and shifting toward broader incentives for economic improvement—would be much more costly for the state in terms of political legitimacy and its alliances with firms. The state, by relying on signals of opportunity, rationally manages its interdependencies with economic elites. And political elites broaden their base of popular support, responding to local chiefs' (and municipal councils') demands for more rapid expansion of education.

Imperative 2: Shaping and Reinforcing Class Interests

In practicing the art of state-craft, political actors must view society in both the first and the third persons. The fragile state is located within a slightly larger concentric circle—the polity. Here state elites act *subjectively* as key members of a small political-economy. Yet the fragile state, eager to deliver on promises of modernity and economic change, must also *objectify* the larger society, especially the problematic outer circle of laborers and rural peasants who reside on the edges of the modern polity and cash economy. The fragile state attempts to lead a large scale project of transforming society and rationalizing its organization. But at the same time, core class interests must be reinforced or recast in ways that do not undercut the legitimacy, cultural ideals, or the material advantages held by economic and political elites.

The state also yearns to burrow into the polity's heart—to be seen subjectively as a necessary, even a "natural" set of civic institutions. When the state overly objectifies society or takes an excessively critical posture, political institutions come to be seen as "ideological" or somehow foreign. Fragile states, especially in Africa, are bound by this dilemma. Political elites may honestly attempt to extend economic development and opportunity to the hinterlands. But when the state moves beyond core economic and ideological commitments, it risks support from central groups within the polity. These core commitments may focus on parastatal enterprises that control agricultural trade, on corporate industrial interests, or on the welfare of the urban civil service. But political actors play with fire when they risk taking a critical perspective on this bundle of class advantages and social ideals resting at the polity's center.[18]

Juggling Class Interests

Malawi's fragile state—and the contested organizational form of schooling—is caught up in this dilemma. Political leaders seek to enfranchise rural villagers while reinforcing forms of schooling that serve narrower class interests. First, let me illuminate those mechanisms, working within educational organizations, which largely reinforce urban elite and (fledgling) middle class interests. These state-determined processes include (a) high differentiation between low-quality (mass) primary schooling versus high-quality, well subsidized secondary and university schooling, (b) a centralized examination and pupil selection system that reinforces urban roles, knowledge and symbols, and (c) the state's limited penetration into, and constrained capacity to boost social demand for schooling in rural areas.

Second, I show how the state *is* trying to attack class advantages and open up educational opportunity. The central education ministry has moved to (a) equalize, between urban and rural areas, the distribution of better trained teachers and school inputs, (b) introduce rural knowledge and symbols into the official curriculum, and (c) democratize access to post-primary levels. Agencies within the state, of course, are not successful on all fronts. Indeed, by rapidly expanding educational opportunity, quality has declined within the mass primary system, inadvertently exacerbating institutional stratification. But state actors are not blind to how elements of the school structure reinforce class advantage.

These bureaucrats and political leaders are (objectively) applying the antidote of "mass opportunity." Whether this medicine is sufficient remains a nagging question.

The State Forms Class Differences

The Malawian state has stuck to its decision to limit mass schooling to the primary level. Entry into secondary school remains highly selective. Many African states have rapidly expanded lower secondary schooling, signaling greater educational opportunity and keeping youths off a typically overcrowded wage-labor market. But Malawi has been more prudent, seeking to conserve resources and recognizing that the wage-sector will continue to grow very slowly. This high selectivity and inequitable levels of subsidy between primary and post-primary institutions serve to reinforce class differences within Malawian society. The simple scarcity of secondary and university degree holders, for example, drives up their status and economic returns.

Just 40 percent of all primary school-age children currently enroll at the beginning of the school year as mentioned above. In rural areas pupil attendance is irregular at best. Only one fifth of all students actually persist through the eight-year primary school cycle and then successfully pass the school-leaving exam. In absolute numbers this equals about 70,000 graduates each year. Secondary school places are available for only 7,500 of these graduates. This 10 percent rate of admission into secondary school has remained the same since the 1970s. Just under two thirds of all entering secondary students are males. Among the 7,500 first-year secondary school pupils, about six hundred will persist through this four-year cycle and enter the University of Malawi. Another eight hundred will eventually enter a teacher training college.[19]

Little is known about the social class background of pupils that persist through primary and secondary school. We do know that school enrollments are higher in urban centers, compared to rural areas. The rate of primary school completion is 10 to 15 percent higher in Malawi's four urban towns, where family cash income is considerably higher, compared to the many more rural districts. Empirical work also reveals the predictable pattern that graduates of teacher training colleges (who have completed some secondary school) come from relatively well-educated families.[20] Interestingly, available evidence shows that acquired literacy of primary school pupils is equal between urban and rural schools, thanks to aggressive state efforts to equalize the distribution of young teachers and school inputs.

State financing patterns clearly advance the interests of those relatively few students who persist into secondary school. At the turn into the 1990s, government allocations to primary school equalled just 28 *kwacha* per pupil or about $10. The bulk of these resources go for teacher salaries. The residual, about 80 cents per pupil, is allocated for textbooks, paper, and exercise booklets. Pupils are expected to have three textbooks each year, provided in part by government and parents, the cost of which equals about $9. In recent years the state has substantially increased spending on basic instructional materials (with support from the World Bank).

State financing for secondary schooling equals about 365 *kwacha* per pupil—thirteen times the subsidy level for primary school students. Stemming from colonial tradition, secondary schools offer boarding facilities which, until recently, were fully subsidized by the state. Spending at the University of Malawi equals about 4,300 *kwacha* for each lucky student—twelve times per-pupil expenditures at the secondary level. Support for each student within teacher training colleges is "only" 1,100 *kwacha* per year. However, these youths become members of the civil service upon entry, draw a stipend, and benefit from fully subsidized boarding facilities.

The school is viewed—by most villagers and town residents—as *the* institution that connects youths to the modern wage-sector. Pushing boys to enter the civic sphere, of course, is more legitimate than encouraging girls to do so. Gender thus becomes a major dimension of class differences. The school does little to rearrange girls' traditional attachments to the household, younger siblings, and the garden plot. Almost half of all children who enter Standard 1 are female. But by Standard 8, girls make up less than a third of pupils enrolled. Achieved literacy of female pupils also falls behind that of boys, with 11 percent fewer girls passing the primary school-leaving exam (as a share of those who sit for it). Unequal access to secondary school also is evident. Just 22 percent of all university students are female. Employment opportunities in education are allocated disproportionately to young men. Two thirds of all primary school teachers are male.[21]

The National Curriculum: Urban Symbols, Restricted Codes

The fragile state typically has a tough time exerting control over the daily actions of headmasters and classroom teachers. But the central state can efficaciously formulate, transmit, and sanction the knowledge and modern symbols that are presented within the classroom. The state employs two basic methods in exercising the symbolic order: mobilizing the national curriculum and relying on standardized examinations to ensure that teachers follow it.

In Malawi the state publishes a curricular timetable that requires headmasters to offer twelve subjects at the primary school level. National textbooks, however, are available for just three subjects: mathematics, English, and Chichewa. To graduate from primary school, pupils must sit for exams in each of these three subjects, plus complete a general paper which covers geography, history, and civics. But, again, only teacher guides exist for these topics, not textbooks for children to study. This does make the national school-leaving exam more difficult to pass, reinforcing its utility as a (seemingly legitimate) selection device. Pupils do not need to pass all subject exams to gain their certificate, except they must pass the English exam. All math textbooks are written in English, since the Chichewa language has limited range when in comes to arithmetic and word problems.

Malawi's national curriculum and standardized tests originally were embedded in the Cambridge examination system, emphasizing the memorization of vocabulary, facts, and figures. Since independence, the state-set curriculum has been broadened a bit. Indeed, reading passages now often touch upon rural forms of authority, culture, and economy. Lessons in measurement or arithmetic more frequently relate to farming and rural trade. Yet the Cambridge influence remains strong: the curriculum places high priority on knowledge and symbols relevant to the modern world, and on the rote memorization of unquestionable "facts." These bits of information often are instructed in highly routinized, authoritarian ways. The teacher stands before the class requiring all pupils to recite a word, sentence, or arithmetic procedure. At times an individual child will be asked to provide the one right answer to a set question. In Chapter 4, we will return to this issue of how routinized pedagogy reinforces the narrow forms of knowledge and codes that the teacher implicitly sanctions.

Let's look, for example, at the initial three problems in the civics portion of the national exam: "Name the civil servant responsible for the collection of taxes"; "Give any two services that are provided by the post office"; "Give the meaning of the police signal given in Figure 1." The figure shows a (rarely seen) traffic cop urging you to halt. Another interesting question on this exam asks "What is money?"

Published textbooks still reinforce modern symbols linked to urban elites, not to the 85 percent of all Malawians living in subsistence villages. The Standard 7 English text, for instance, has a unit entitled, "The clothes people wear." Pictured at the top of the passage is a man wearing a suit and necktie; the woman is dressed in a modest skirt and blouse with a bow. Flipping through the 150-page Standard 5 English text, the pictures are instructive: one finds pictures of a factory, a tobacco warehouse, a supermarket, a family talking within a Western house, pets sleeping in beds, and illustrations of London.[22]

Not all information and symbols transmitted through the curriculum are linked to urban forms. Reading passages and arithmetic problems do occasionally relate to life in the village: including cultural practices, moral lessons, and practical concerns of production, exchange, health, and nutrition. Western-sponsored textbook writers, and increasingly their Malawian colleagues, *are* attempting to move "official knowledge" closer to practical problems which face rural communities.

Despite this pursuit of more balanced content, however, the form of knowledge and codes remains quite narrow. Simply working in the written word acts to "de-contextualize" the knowledge that is sanctioned by the formal school (to use psychologist Lev Vygotsky's term).[23] That is, children must memorize pieces of information and facts that are quite independent of their daily contexts. This form of literacy and numeracy, being so foreign to children's settings, does serve the state's interest in selecting the few who make it into the modern-sector. The process is rational in terms of legitimating the state's authority in, and means by which, the modern polity pulls-in a few more members. But the narrow type of literacy and learning offered does little to advance forms of knowledge or problem-solving capacity that would serve rural peoples. And even for urban youth, these restricted codes hammered into kids' heads contribute little to building basic reasoning capacity. Knowledge is viewed as a finite commodity that is delivered on a plate and either swallowed or not. In Malawi, people talk about being "educated" or being "backward" (that is, not having swallowed the schooling treatment).

Combating Urban-Rural Inequities

Class distinctions are not set in stone. The forming of class interests, within particular groups located in similar situations, is a process that unfolds over time. As productive, commercial, and social institutions change, the boundaries of classes and communities shift. The fragile state often plays a role, even inadvertently, in shaping categories of individuals and in building the institutions that define communities of interest. The inequities faced by rural peoples in Malawi are obvious, even to state actors who are conditioned to act cautiously and without a visibly critical perspective. Yet, importantly, the state is moving to equalize the distribution of new teachers and basic instructional materials.

Recent research, for instance, shows that teachers' own literacy and numeracy is often higher in rural primary schools than in urban schools. The rural teaching force is a bifurcated set of two groups. Older male teachers entered their school posts not long after independence and possess high status in their communities. The second group is composed of recent graduates of teacher training college who must, according to state requirements, teach in rural areas for several years. These new teachers persisted longer through secondary school and received more pre-service training than their older colleagues. In addition, class sizes tend to be substantially lower in rural areas, in part due to lower attendance rates. One recent study found that the average class size in rural primary schools equalled just twenty-nine pupils, compared to eighty-five students in urban classrooms. Importantly, this same work shows that supplies of textbooks, teacher curricular guides, and pupil exercise books are greater (on a per pupil basis) within rural schools.[24]

As a result pupil achievement in rural areas appears to converge with urban achievement by the end of the primary school cycle. This is partially explained by the fact that many more rural youths drop out of school before reaching Standard 8. Those that persist must be unusually motivated or pushed strongly by their family and village. Yet the evidence remains that both math and Chichewa scores are roughly equal for rural and urban pupils. Literacy in Chichewa is far lower among rural Standard 3 students; but those that persist through Standard 8 catch up with their urban counterparts. Chichewa is a foreign language for about half of all Malawian children when they enter school. Teachers must often speak in the local tribal language (when they know it) over the first two or three grade levels. In contrast, rural math scores equal urban scores as early as Standard 3. Since math is taught in English, less urban advantage is present. But urban children are at an advantage in learning Chichewa, since this is the Malawian *lingua franca* spoken among Malawian elites within the private sector and the civil service.[25]

Imperative 3: Advancing Teachers' Interests

Post-colonial states actively support and shape one major class of wage earners: civil servants. Government employees in many African countries comprise 70 percent of the entire wage-sector or more. Teachers usually make up the majority of the civil service. And at times the social welfare and employment function of mass schooling preoccupies state actors, not the technical task of boosting children's literacy. In Malawi, for instance, over 90 percent of all recurrent spending on primary schools goes for salaries of teachers or school administrators. Only the remaining residual is available for essential instructional materials. Teachers' wages in Africa, despite recent economic shocks, remain quite competitive. Yet the price teachers pay is that the state, then, has few resources to print textbooks or provide basic writing materials.[26]

State actors face two painful dilemmas as they attempt to protect the interests of this class of white-collar workers. First, pressure on the state to expand mass schooling necessitates the training of more teachers, further thinning out government resources that could otherwise go into wage increases for incumbent teachers. Second, as formal schooling becomes a *mass* institution, the status of teaching declines. As enrollments expand more rapidly than state resources, classrooms become more crowded and basic teaching tools become more scarce. Basic working conditions, particularly in over crowded urban schools, become undesirable, even dismal. Immediately after independence, teachers were in great demand; teaching was one of the few wage-earning jobs available to well-schooled Africans. But rapid expansion requires lowering entry standards for new teachers, cutting corners in how young teachers are prepared. The literate teacher is still an esteemed role in much of Africa. But literacy *per se* no longer holds the revered status that it once held. Literate youths, in some cases, can now pursue other job opportunities in a (slow growing) wage-sector.

New teachers face mixed levels of pay, status, and working conditions. In poor nations, like Malawi, keep in mind that the wage-sector is quite small. Few options exist outside the civil service. A new teacher in Malawi typically has completed four years of secondary schooling, plus two years of pre-service training. Teachers with this level of preparation and civil service grade can earn between 1,200 and 3,800 *kwacha* each year. As mentioned above, the average Malawian teacher earns the equivalent of $800 annually. This wage is comparable to what stenographers and typists earn within the civil service. It is considerably greater than the average wages of carpenters, government nurses and midwives, and secretaries. Teachers earn about one third of what the government pays engineers and doctors. In Malawi, the teacher's annual pay is bumped up automatically each year. This increment equals about $1.50 per month. The overall salary structure is adjusted upward every 5 to 7 years—during which time inflation typically rises 50 to 100 percent.[27]

Working Conditions in a Mass Institution

The erosion of working conditions is a major concern of teachers in Malawi. This cuts into perceived status, lowers their morale, and fuels greater pressure on the state to address teachers' class interests. Our survey of 130 teachers included questions regarding their backgrounds and working conditions. The sample was split evenly among teachers working in Standards 3, 4, and 7. Contrasts between teachers working in rural versus urban schools are especially important to understand.

First, teachers are now relatively advantaged, although most originally came from traditional villages. They are an upwardly mobile lot. About 80 percent grew up in thatch-roof huts. Many of their fathers did employ basic literacy in their work. Forty percent of the rural, and 50 percent of the urban, teachers completed secondary school. The majority of urban teachers are female. This is largely due to the fact that wives of male civil servants receive preference for urban teaching jobs when their husband is transfer into the city.

Second, teaching conditions are tough, particularly within urban schools. Here class sizes average eighty-five pupils. Surveyed teachers received just thirty-five textbooks on average during the current school year. With a published text for each of three subjects, a complete set for eighty-five pupils would equal 255 texts. The majority of pupils sit on the floor, given the scarcity of desks, in both rural and urban schools.

Third, teachers appear to work quite autonomously within their classrooms. They reported that their headmasters observed their teaching practices less than three times over the past three years! Visits by school inspectors reportedly were even less frequent. Some interaction with parents was indicated by teachers. But even this communication is infrequent, given the large number of pupils each teacher oversees.

In sum, teachers have personally experienced mobility and opportunity, moving from the village to secure a wage-earning job and higher status based on their position and literacy. But the rapid expansion of schooling undercuts their working conditions and status, boosting the number of children they face in the classroom, constraining wage increases, and steadily diminishing even basic teaching tools. As teachers become more organized, pressure intensifies on the state to respond to and reinforce their class interests.

Imperative 4: Modern (Bureaucratic) Management

The district education officer (DEO) faced a painful predicament when the sobbing teacher called. The teacher's uncle had just died, some 40 kilometers away, far to the south of Zomba. But the DEO's only Land Rover was in the government repair shop, having vanished into that automotive black hole from which few vehicles emerge (at least in less than 6 months time). The DEO, acting under a peculiar mix of state regulation and government tradition, was obliged to move the body to the preferred burial ground. (Distribution of teacher salaries and textbooks must wait under such a situation.) As the education ministry's representative, the DEO must respect this entitlement and protect the government's credibility. Fortunately, he worked out a deal to borrow the health clinic's Land Rover and was off in a flash to meet the grieving teacher.

The state's first management priority is to penetrate into local areas, to signal that "government" is at least present and watching over local schools. A network of three regional and over twenty district education offices sit between the central education ministry and Malawi's 1,800 primary schools. Similar to the old British form of school administration, each DEO employs several inspectors—circuit riders who move around the bush or urban neighborhoods checking on schools. This form of modern management, until quite recently, did little to improve the behavior of teachers in the classroom. However, district supervision does serve to routinize what headmasters do, and how they see their own role at the school level.

Routinization of the headmaster's job and selective coupling along specific lines—even simple signals of "good management"—are reassuring. Uncertainty and exigencies at the school level are enormous: pupil attendance is irregular, and drop-out rates are high; instructional materials don't show up due to fuel shortages; pay checks come late, usually requiring the headmaster to take the bus or hitch-hike to the DEO's office; a political figure may be visiting the region, requiring teachers to organize youthful well-wishers and dancers. One way to combat uncertainty locally is to express signals of control and supervision centrally. This is a major element of effective state-craft, whether we are looking at fragile Third World states or established states in the First World. International donors often press fragile states to display techniques of "modern management": hierarchical control, routinization and prescription of technical tasks, constant evaluation and supervision from above. (Of course, many Western firms and organizations have abandoned these Weberian forms of administration.)

So local agents of the state—especially school inspectors—drop down lines of control, hoping to press order upon the school headmaster's work. Inspectors in Malawi focus upon an interesting set of tasks or facets of the school organization. They must fill out a standard form when they visit a school which requires inspection of the following items:

Headmaster

1. Records are of principal importance, including those related to the class schedule, enrollments and student fees collected, teaching staff and daily attendance, budget accounts, and a listing of visitors to the school.
2. The headmaster's office is commonly checked for its tidiness and appearance, and whether recent circulars from the ministry are properly posted.

Teachers

3. Many inspectors check to see if teachers are handing in their abbreviated lesson plans for the headmaster's review. These plans outline the content of lessons to be presented over a week's period, sometimes daily lessons are required.

4. Inspectors may visit a few classrooms to assess the availability of textbooks, teacher curricular guides, and paper.

Buildings and grounds

5. Much time is spent surveying the grounds, checking on the school garden, footpaths, flower beds, and playing fields.
6. Latrines are a major concern, since they often are overflowing, filthy, and act as a major source of bacterial disease.
7. Classrooms and teachers' houses (owned by the government) are checked to see if the thatch or sheet-metal roofs are effective, walls are clean, and windows are intact (the glass panes are rarely present).[28]

Inspectors attend to problems that parents or village leaders may point out. The DEO is the main political pressure point when the village leadership becomes frustrated over a teacher with irregular attendance, infrequent delivery of textbooks, or the lack of government support in repairing crumbling classrooms. Local school committees provide input to the headmaster and DEO and allocate a share of revenues generated by student fees. Headmasters and DEOs must approach the school committee to organize brick making and construction of additional classrooms or teacher housing. The DEO's own position is threatened if he or she can not adequately respond to, or mobilize, village chiefs and local parents. Thus the DEO's process of selective coupling must include a response to particular local demands and grievances.

Each school inspector hopes to visit between thirty and one hundred schools each year. In rural areas of Malawi, an inspector may take a day-long bus ride, then walk another day to reach a remote school. So no time exists for follow-up on these problem areas. The inspector works from a checklist; he or she may provide basic advice. Then, the inspector moves on to the next school. The headmaster, individual teacher, or local school committee must decide whether sufficient material or technical resources exist to remedy the weaknesses identified by this traveling agent of the state.

Inventive Local Management

Thus far in this story, the Malawian state seems more concerned with demonstrating symbols of modern (bureaucratic) management than in improving teaching and learning within the classroom. This would not, however, be a complete portrayal of the education ministry's selective links with local schools. Beginning in the mid-1980s, the central ministry began to discuss how teachers could receive better guidance and ongoing feedback on their pedagogical practices. Two important efforts have developed from these constructively critical discussions.

First, the Malawi Institute of Education received donor support from UNICEF to draft a modest handbook on alternative teaching methods. This 165-page pocketbook urges teachers to move away from exclusive reliance on the old colonial "chalk-and-talk" method of instruction. Simple pedagogical innovations are described, including ways of asking children more questions, using demonstration and role-playing techniques, and employing cooperative learning groups. Distributed by the education ministry and the parastatal book publisher, this handbook has become a best-seller. Occasionally one can even see teachers experimenting with these new pedagogical techniques.[29]

Second, the education ministry and institute developed a training program for DEOs, inspectors, and headmasters that imparts to these local managers how to encourage better teaching practices in the classroom. This extensive retooling occurs over a 2-year period of study. Simple tools have been developed to reinforce this broader role for these local school managers. For example, classroom observation forms have been developed to help provide constructive feedback to teachers. Based on interviews with inspectors, these simple devices are in fact employed by many. The habit to control those behaviors that can possibly be codified and routinized is strong, often subverting the best of intentions. Even those inspectors who have taken on the role of "instructional leader" rather than "regulator," still often focus on how well the teacher has recorded his or her instructional objectives and lesson plans, not whether the teacher is motivating children.[30]

Yet, my cursory review of inspection reports written by recent graduates of the school management training program reveals that a new role is being assumed. These younger inspectors spend less time on aspects of organizational maintenance and more time in classrooms providing feedback about pedagogy. A sampling of comments to teachers:

"Discourage pupils from giving echo (choral) answers to your questions."

"Pupils should use new words in a sentence of their own."

"Continue to give special assistance to backward pupils."

"Break topics into more teachable units."

"Pupils should be actively involved in the lesson through questions or other activities."[31]

Much work remains to be done. Inspectors and headmasters may provide unclear or counterproductive feedback in some cases. The routinization of "good teaching" and its codification on to a new form may stifle certain pedagogical skills and styles. Social rules inherent within some observation protocols may conflict with traditional views of the teacher's authority and expertise. Yet this remarkable action by the Malawian state and its educational leaders leads us to two interrelated points.

First, the state is beginning to change the role of local school managers, moving sharply away from traditional forms of bureaucratic management and symbolic displays of order. The state is not urging compliance with this new role of "instructional leader." Instead, the state is *illustrating* how this new set of behaviors can improve the quality of pedagogy. This is done through careful (re)training, simple tools, and recruitment of younger inspectors and headmasters who are open to new forms of management and school improvement.

Second, the state (indirectly) is showing a capacity to influence the actions and scripts followed by the teacher within the classroom. Earlier researchers, working within the loose-coupling tradition, argued that local school staff will consistently buffer state actors in the latter's attempts to alter what goes on in classrooms. At first glance, the fragile Malawian state appears to follow this pattern. Struggling to exercise modern management, state actors are satisfied with selective coupling along the material controllable facets of the school organization. But checking the condition of latrines is far from improving the quality of teaching. State actors are not dumb; they can see this. In the case of Malawi, local agents of the state have moved further to penetrate the classroom's walls, nudging teachers to change their behavior and beliefs. This occasional efficacy, of course, advances the state's interest in deepening the effects of mass schooling.

Summary: The State as Struggling Sculptor

Actors within the state, be they political leaders or education bureau-crats, constantly attempt to wind up the school institution and send it careening in a particular direction. The state must muster sufficient resources to build more schools and to hire more teachers. It mobilizes administrative devices to train teachers, produce textbooks, and create and enforce selection and allocation mechanisms, like national exams. Most importantly, the state acts symbolically to sanction the school institution as *the* modern way of socializing one's children.

The fragile state, like the struggling sculptor, must work hard simply to craft and animate the skeletal form. The addition of texture and detail, of character and expression, is even more difficult. The state is required to sculpt the role and behavior of the classroom teacher. State actors also invent and enforce the basic instructional tools made available. Only through these channels can political agencies hope to deepen the school's effect on children. But the state is bounded by clear constraints and uncertainties—in its material resources, administrative efficacy, technical know-how, and capacity to symbolically penetrate local com-munities and traditional commitments.

The political sculptor, though engaged in expressive state-craft, must respond to four strong imperatives:

- To signal mass opportunity
- To shape and reinforce class interests
- To advance the interests of teachers
- To employ modern (bureaucratic) forms of management

However, each imperative—rooted in Western beliefs about the state's legitimate role and social ideals—presents serious contradictions for the fragile state. Popular expectations for greater opportunity encourage political elites to rapidly expand mass schooling. But even as a signaling device, it is costly, straining the state's scarce resources. The state must enhance the economic and cultural interests of urban elites. Yet Western traditions require political leaders to incorporate the hinterlands, even respect plural cultural interests. This requires rethinking of how a homog-enous school structure and content can become more attractive to rural families. And when Weberian forms of centralized management have little effect on teacher motivation or student achievement, modern images of how to regulate schools begin to dissolve. Political actors may share a common vision of where they are headed. But the constraints and contradictions surrounding these heartfelt imperatives often bump state actors way off course.

The fragile Third World state struggles to look more modern—to integrate a disparate nation-state, to build Western-like institutions, and to broaden mass opportunity. Each day pre-modern realities beset well-meaning political elites: feudal economic interests resist a press for market structures, limited infrastructure constrains government penetration into rural areas or urban shantytowns, and local village chiefs resist government education policies. So, state actors redouble their resolve and mount innovative strategies for consolidating material and social capital, for adjusting local administration, and for recasting signals and advocacy of modernity as expressed through the daily newspapers. The faith-filled mission of the fragile state is to conquer these pre-modern forces.

This ecumenical dialectic, where darkness equals tradition and light is represented by modernity, traps the state. The demands and contradictions that paralyze it are defined by this dialectic. The fragile state must attempt to deepen the school's effect, for example. Within Western corporate forms of organization, the state can best signal efficacy by routinizing the teacher's role and behavior, and by homogenizing and reducing the form of knowledge found within the classroom. Thus we observe efforts to standardize curricula, teaching practices, and national exams.

This movement toward more modern organizational forms signifies that the state is a competent actor and that the school will more clearly serve the integrated nation-state's uniform interests. For a more gentle state to respect plural differences of local communities, or to pursue more creative ways of motivating teachers, comes to be seen as a hazy, unmodern approach. It implies that the state does not hold the magical remedy for developing its youth. For if the state can not define a common form of schooling and teaching, how can it expect its children to grow up modern?

4

Strong States, Strong Teachers?

My friend Chimtali, age 14, moved 10 kilometers from her small village nestled against the Zomba plateau to just outside the trading post of the same name. She had recently entered a government boarding school to pursue her secondary studies. She liked her teachers and her subjects. It was the foreign-seeming customs that she found amusing. Chimtali now was required to wear pajamas at night. And she was relearning how to eat. Growing up in the village she simply used her hands, but now she was required to use utensils imported from London. Nor was she allowed to eat fried *ngumbi*, those plentiful and tasty African bugs resembling winged roaches. While Chimtali obviously enjoyed becoming modern, she had not suspected that secondary school would require such deep changes in daily habits.

To this point, we have focused on how the state attempts to be strong. Political actors and education bureaucrats, for example, are eager to expand mass schooling and to craft the teacher's role and tools. But in reality how efficacious are state actors in shaping life *inside classrooms* and in deepening the school's effect on children? This chapter tackles this question, focusing on how the teacher organizes work and action within the classroom.

In Chapter 3, we looked at the organizational levers that central actors push and pull as they pursue the state's political imperatives. But contradictions are immediately confronted: (1) the pursuit of mass opportunity and mass schooling runs into the state's fiscal and adminis-trative constraints; (2) political elites must first serve urban interests and friends, despite urgent demands to transform the rural economy; (3) rapid growth of mass schooling relentlessly erodes the status and working conditions of teachers, undercutting intended social and economic effects; and (4) a frustrated state intensifies control and routinizes the teacher's role and knowledge transmitted into the classroom. These imperatives and dilemmas emanate from central government. But how are they played out within local schools and classrooms? When are these institution-level actions, exercised by the state, more likely felt by teachers and children?

Let's pose the question strongly: Does the classroom teacher act as a messenger for the central state, conveying political actors' preferred social rules, knowledge, and moral symbols? To answer the question we will be looking inside African classrooms, observing the actions and beliefs of teachers who work under the centralized Malawian state. We will be asking whether, and how, state actions shape the role, behavior, and beliefs of local teachers. This large issue can be broken down into three specific questions.

First: *Does the school function as a factory or as a religion?* Does the teacher mechanically deliver the rules and beliefs sanctioned by state actors, and do so within a *rationally administered* school organization? Or does the school operate as an institution independently of the central state, held together by shared *religious-like* ideals, symbols, and rituals of membership? Here the teacher would act to signal his or her authority within a bounded institution, not as a messenger anxious to conform to the state's intentions. Nor would the teacher necessarily act in ways which boost the school's influence on children.

Second: *Do schools primarily display resistance or institutionalized acceptance?* The formal school has gained widespread, popular acceptance as the modern *location* for socializing children. But is institutionalized faith in the central state sufficiently strong so that teachers acquiesce to the demands of political actors, especially in terms of the classroom's *content* and social rules? We review the lively debate on whether pupils (even within industrialized nations) actively resist forms of control which are seen as factory-like and obtrusive. Perhaps most children simply accept the moral order and unobtrusive social rules exercised by teachers and headmasters.

Third: *how do teachers control classroom action?* Messengers, to speak effectively to disbelieving or indifferent listeners, must negotiate and construct palpable meanings. At a broad level, the central state can legitimate the school as the place for socializing youngsters, claiming that the magic of modern instruction results in better jobs, self-enrichment, or greater equality. Yet when children enter the classroom for the first time, they confront a foreign bureaucracy, replete with knowledge and symbols that must be interpreted (assigned meaning) by the teacher. When pupils respond with resistance or simple disinterest, the teacher employs various means to boost their loyalty to classroom rules and curricular content. To understand the teacher's particular role vis-a-vis the central state, we must examine the processes by which he or she draws on the school's authority and resources to deepen effects on pupils. These strategies involve mobilization of material resources (such as, how instructional materials are utilized), direct control of pupils' behavior, and less obtrusive modeling of a bureaucratic moral order.[1] As we will see, the teacher also must accommodate the diversity and indifference of pupils if his or her authority is to be preserved.

After reviewing competing theoretical viewpoints, we will peer into the lively world of African classrooms. I start from a strong-state position, claiming that the *teacher's authority*, *role*, *and tools* are determined by elites from within the formal polity. These actors include political elites within ministries of education; but we must also include local civic leaders and economic elites who press teachers to behave in certain ways, to instruct certain knowledge and social rules. In the southern African nation of Malawi, as in other settings, these elites are united by their earnest desire to deepen the school's influence on how children are socialized.

Counterposed to this "teacher as state messenger" claim are the three issues introduced above. When we focus on the teacher's actual behavior and beliefs, correspondence with the state's explicit agenda comes into question. The school's insular, religious-like form of authority, pupil diversity and indifference, and the teacher's own methods for patterning action in the classroom may all prompt divergence from the state's narrower aims. We will see that in some settings the teacher does not simply respond to the central state's wishes; nor do pupils passively internalize the explicit curriculum and implicit moral order found in African classrooms. This will lead us to a more textured and situational view of when strong states breed strong teachers . . . as opposed to when the teacher operates from an autonomous position. I will then ask whether the state's influence actually stems more from its unintended creation of mass conditions inside the classroom, rather than from its blunt, more clumsy attempts at administrative control.

Does the Central State Touch the Teacher?

In Chapter 2, I reviewed competing models put forward to explain both the expansion and the deepening of mass schooling. To give order to my observations in African classrooms, I return to these alternative theories. In Figure 4.1 the three major issues linked to the *teacher's role* within a strong state are specified as row headings. Columns are defined by the three explanations of why and how the state attempts to deepen the school's effect on children.

Each theory attempts to link state action with the teacher's role in the classroom. But the models differ sharply in terms of (a) what specific actions within the classroom we should focus on; and (b) the meaning or interpretation assigned to these behaviors, beliefs, and their subsequent effects on pupils. The *bureaucratic version* of the *functional-modernity* model, for instance, emphasizes how the teacher should inculcate modern attitudes in pupils—preaching the virtues of Western knowledge, science, differentiated and specialized labor, and self-conscious regulation of production and social life. From Durkheim's or Comte's original functionalist perspective, the teacher is seen as an agent of, and manipulated by, the central state, socializing "traditional" children to see the advantages of modern progress.[2]

The *ideological version* of functionalist thought stresses the moral or sacred social rules that should be explicitly taught or implicitly transmitted by the teacher. In the United States, for example, this includes teaching children that they should value individualistic forms of achievement, and that performance will be judged by impersonal authorities (teachers and tests) which are rooted in a bureaucratic institution. Within the mass school, children also are taught that formal authorities can legitimately define the nature of one's work, and that work itself is something that is extrinsically rewarded by another, not something that should hold intrinsic value for the child.

Both versions of functionalist theory see a tight correspondence between the central state and the teacher's action; and this close link is interpreted as a positive process by which the polity's values are reproduced and the "common good" is consolidated and reinforced.

From the *class imposition* viewpoint, the school operates much like a factory with regard to pupils. Children of the elite and many middle class pupils are socialized with an emphasis on individual autonomy

Figure 4.1   The State and Teacher Action: Competing Theories

Basic Issues	Functional-Modernity	Class Imposition	World Institutions
ISSUE 1 State/school correspondence? —School boundaries and structure	School fits nicely with social rules of state and economic bureaucracies; school's boundaries are permeable.	"School-as-factory" theories see fit between corporate and school bureaucracies; "oft-autonomous" theorists argue that school boundaries buffer pressure for hegemony, allowing counter ideals to grow.	School institution is a tight legitimate movement that serves the Western state's material and political ideals; school organization internally operates as a religious institution, patterned by shared symbols, not rational controls.
—Classroom rules	Teacher holds strong authority and must focus on maintaining order and loyalty of pupils within mass schools; in turn teacher works in a hierarchical structure and is expected to conform (unprofessionally) to dictates from the headmaster or state actors.	Rules differ by social class of pupil; factory-like organization of labor for working-class kids vs. independence and more complex knowledge for middle-class pupils; "oft-autonomous" theorists argue that counter social rules can develop.	Teacher signals membership in the school organization, acts in ways which preserve his/her own authority, and responds symbolically, not materially, to bureaucratic controls from above.
—Moral order	Teacher socializes children to achieve within mass bureaucratic settings: universal, highly specific forms of merit are rewarded: teacher encourages individualistic and competitive performance on routinized tasks/knowledge.	Agree with functionalist view, but class theorists claim that this moral order serves the interests of elites, alienating children from intrinsic rewards and control over their own learning and labor.	Teachers and pupils join the modern polity and signal acceptance of the state structure by participating in the secular school; sign of membership is most fundamental, not reductionist task of raising achievement.
ISSUE 2 Teacher and pupil resistance?	Teacher performance can be raised by "improved management," that is tighter rational controls, routinization of knowledge and teaching, evaluation of teacher's actions; pupil indifference attacked by stiffer "standards" or more sophisticated strategies for boosting loyalty to the school institution.	"School-as-factory" theorists see considerable resistance by pupils (and teachers); whereas "structuralist" theorists see general acceptance of the school's social rules and moral order; "oft-autonomous" theorists view growth of counter ideals as a successful form of resistance.	Little resistance, mass popular support for expansion and deepening of Western schooling found throughout modern polities.
ISSUE 3 Teacher's methods of control	Teacher attempts greater social control and higher pupil performance through positive and negative rewards; teacher also assigns sacred meaning to modern knowledge, character traits, and classroom rules.	Teacher controls pupils in classic bureaucratic ways; encouraging individual competition, routinizing tasks, and allocating extrinsic rewards; the teacher must constantly seek to reinforce his/her own authority.	By acting in legitimate ways the teacher reinforces his/her own authority and invites the child to signal membership and performance in the classroom.
INTERPRETIVE EMPHASIS	Correspondence between state and school organizations and their moral tenets—a consonance achieved through bureaucratic control and signals of membership in modern organization.	Correspondence between elites' agenda and the social rules of the classroom; differential social rules in the classroom also reinforce class inequality.	Broad support for schooling by the masses and political elites; from the outside, school institution signals "modern progress"; inside, school's order is religious/symbolic and not bureaucratic.

Note: References appear in endnotes for chapters 2 and 4.

and broader intellectual skills. Working-class or peasant children, in contrast, are fit into routine types of instruction and controlled in more obtrusive ways. This differential form of classroom control and tracking helps legitimate and reinforce inequality in the larger society. Recent ethnographic studies reveal that low-status pupils often resist such bureaucratic forms of socialization. Yet their rebellion rarely affects the classroom structure, only serving to differentiate stigmatized working-class kids from more conforming children who have internalized the school's moral precepts.[3]

Similar to functional theorists, European structuralists emphasize that all pupils, regardless of class, are socialized to accept the moral order upon which Western bureaucracies are founded, organizations dedicated to the dominant political order and to economic expansion. However, the school institution may sprout ideals and moral beliefs that run counter to dominant ideologies of the central state. In recent writings, for instance, Michael Apple, Martin Carnoy, and Henry Giroux each argue that teachers may encourage cooperative or creative action by pupils, not only competitive and homogenous forms. Or teachers may point out that altruistic and democratic values taught in literature and textbooks often conflict with the realities of political action. Here the teacher and school, within limits, modestly resist the central state's official agenda.[4]

The *world institution* perspective emphasizes how the central state extends membership in the modern polity through the mass school. But John W. Meyer and colleagues also argue that the secular school was institutionalized quite early within core European countries and has gained instant legitimacy within newly independent Third World polities (as reviewed in Chapter 2). Thus, while central political or economic elites often attempt to mobilize the school's material and symbolic resources, the school institution is encased in a rather impermeable skin. Like a monk in a monastery, the teacher engages in a variety of actions and expressive beliefs that signal solidarity with the institution's own faith and ideals—but which may not correspond to the state's preferred rules. For example, Meyer points out that teachers relentlessly stand before pupils and lecture at them, despite recurrent pleas by teacher educators and researchers that such practices are ineffective. Such actions are entirely rational in signaling the teacher's authority and membership within the religion of mass schooling. Whether membership rituals actually help boost pupils' achieved literacy is another question.[5]

Cutting Loose the Central State?

The major question underlying all three theories is whether the teacher accepts and acts from the central state's agenda, or whether the teacher resists (or is simply indifferent to) the ideals and controls exercised by political elites. After reporting on life within African classrooms, I will argue that correspondence between the central state and the local teacher begins to break down due to three factors: pupil indifference, unclear and inconsistent signals from the central state, and mixed beliefs held by teachers regarding their own role and normative behavior within the mass school. As Hegel pointed out, central states will attempt to muffle the clanging of local particularities. Political elites do this by arguing for a shared faith in universal ideals: rationality and Western forms of knowledge, a common language, economic integration and expansion. But in much of the Third World, local economic forms and cultural patterns persist, mitigating against the fragile state's efforts to penetrate and transform communities.[6]

This recurring *detachment from the central state* pushes political elites to reassess their interdependencies and methods of influencing local actors. The teacher is clearly the bearer of Western faith. But this faith, as passed down from central elites is a haphazard bundle of modern symbols, often with little internal logic. The school institution has its own traditions, habits, and signals of membership—at times complementing, at times conflicting with, the central state's desire for broader incorporation. It is this push and pull between the state and the school which I emphasize. At times the teacher gains status and material resources by aligning himself or herself with the central state's agenda (look at the current state-sanctioned craze over bringing modern computers into the classroom). Yet other times the teacher expresses the school institution's distinct forms of authority and ideology, or the teacher must devise inventive strategies for motivating indifferent pupils within mass classroom settings.

So, the southern African teacher is told to speak English or the official (that is, the dominant tribal) language in the classroom. But with thirty-five different tribes in Malawi, for instance, many children would understand little of what the teacher was saying. To maintain control and authority in the classroom, the teacher must be accommodating. It is this process of mutual accommodation that becomes so clear as one sits in the back of Third World classrooms. The state's largely convergent and homogenous agenda—in terms of boosting Western knowledge, social rules, and moral tenets—confronts local conditions marked by diversity, resistance, and passive indifference (especially in the Third World).

We should better specify those cases when, and the means by which, the central state successfully muffles the sound of these clashing symbols inherent in local diversity. Focusing on the teacher, I ask, when does the teacher aid and abet this convergent agenda of the state, and when does the teacher act from counter rules, beliefs, and symbols which implicitly challenge the state?

Describing the Action of Teachers

Modern political elites, including central actors and local school leaders, get very nervous when they perceive that teachers are detached from the state's ideals. In the United States, for instance, recurring anxiety over low and declining pupil achievement has led to sharp administrative reforms and a good deal of research on how the school's effect on children can be deepened. Questions about what teachers actually do in classrooms are driven by the state's and the broader polity's concern that children are not learning enough. So researchers look inside the classroom, attempting to link certain teacher behaviors with higher student achievement. The content and form of knowledge to be learned is not questioned; nor are the social rules examined within which the teacher imparts these codes. Desired achievement outcomes are simply passed down by school elders as sacred, unquestioned "social facts." Thus the normative researcher engages in the instrumental technical task of discovering how teacher action in the classroom can deepen orthodox forms of pupil virtue (measured by standard exams tapping retention of vocabulary, grammar, arithmetic, or civics).

Functional versus Critical Views of the Classroom

At a technical and *functional* level, reports of teachers' classroom action have contributed important pieces of evidence. Early research in classrooms by Jane Stallings in the United States, for instance, revealed that many teachers spend an enormous amount of time simply organizing lessons, grading homework, and disciplining pupils—rather than actually delivering instruction. For instance, one study found that pupils spend only about 38 percent of a typical school day actually engaged in academic tasks. A more recent study, also done in the United States, confirmed that some teachers spend less than half of each class period actually involved in instructional tasks. Subsequent work both in Britain and the United States has documented that the amount of time teachers spend engaged in academic tasks does influence levels of pupil achievement. At least one state government now actually certifies new teachers based on observed proficiencies in "minimizing time spent on noninstructional activities, clarity of lesson structure, citing (behavioral) rules when students disobey them, and moving about the classroom and constantly scanning it."[7]

Such observational studies focus exclusively on the technical link between teacher behavior and pupil achievement, given the sacred definition of "achievement" (emphasizing retention of facts and useful pieces of knowledge). Rarely do analysts assume a critical posture and ask: As adoration for tighter teacher controls and routinization of lessons intensifies, what social rules and forms of intellectual action are being taught? Ignoring such normative issues leads to (almost) funny clashes between scientifically-derived findings and a culture's own priorities. Psychologists Harold Stevenson and James Stigler, for instance, recently completed a technically exquisite study of teaching practices in the United States, Taiwan, and Japan. Similar to previous work, they estimated that sampled North American teachers spent 19 hours per week, on average, engaging pupils in academic tasks (after subtracting time spent on classroom management, discipline, and pupil time spent goofing-off). In contrast, Japanese teachers had pupils working on academic tasks 40 hours per week. During this "time-on-task," Japanese teachers were leading the class 70 percent of the time, versus less than half the time in the United States, where 47 percent of instructional time was spent with students individually working at their seats with little interaction taking place.[8]

Stevenson and Stigler's message is that Japanese teachers run tighter classrooms, act more strongly in leading lessons, and demand greater attention from their pupils. If the state's goal is to deepen the school's effect—in terms of raising social conformity and the learning of simple pieces of knowledge—then this *apparent* Japanese strategy should be replicated in other nations. Ironically, however, these messages from United States researchers come at the precise time that many Japanese political leaders and scholars are encouraging greater creativity among pupils and a narrower role for classroom teachers. In addition, other researchers argue that early schooling in Japan holds a deep effect due to the teacher's subtle practice of receding into the background, delegating authority to and expecting responsible action from cooperative work groups.[9]

Socialization in (and for) Mass Organizations

Let's turn to *critical* studies of teachers' action, completing our theoretical backdrop to life inside African classrooms. I have mentioned two key findings that come from functional studies of teacher behavior. First, both teachers and pupils spend a lot of time disengaged from instructional tasks. Second, when teachers are placing academic demands on kids, "teaching" is usually defined either as (a) lecturing at pupils with teachers asking questions of the entire class or an individual child, or (b) assigning seat-work whereby pupils work silently on a uniform task.

Importantly, these two patterns are particularly common in Third World settings. Recent studies in Nigeria and Thailand found that in over two thirds of all classroom snapshots, teachers were simply lecturing at children. During much of the remaining time, pupils were sitting alone (on the floor or at desks) working on assigned exercises. When teachers spoke or queried pupils, these utterances were most often directed at the entire class, not spoken to an individual student. Teachers' questions usually demanded recall of a piece of information, rarely asking for more complex knowledge or pupils' own ideas.[10]

A third finding, emphasized by critical observers of teachers, is that lower-status pupils often are treated differently than high-status students. Researchers Jean Carew and Sara Lawrence Lightfoot, working in United States classrooms, found that teachers tend to interact less with ethnic minority youngsters, compared to high achieving or white children. When teachers did interact with a low-status pupil, the teacher's communication was more often a directive linked to procedures, rather than an inquiry related to academic subject matter or an elicitation of the student's own views. Looking at how pupils are arranged into curriculum tracks, Jeannie Oakes found that they reflected different ways in which low-status versus high-status pupils are socialized in mass schools. Based on classroom observations, she found that low-status pupils were less often engaged in academic tasks, messages from teachers were more often punitive in nature, and pupils reported higher levels of alienation from the teacher.[11]

Critical ethnographies elaborate the latter point, showing that working-class kids are far less integrated into the work and ideology of the classroom, often times actively resisting the teacher's socialization pressures. Teachers' requests for support from parents—to help with homework or to attend school meetings—receive variable responses, depending on parents' social class (manifest in their level of schooling, free time, and resources).[12]

Interpretative analysts emphasize how this differential treatment of children by teachers serves to reinforce class inequality. Within industrialized countries middle class children and offspring of the elite receive more attention from the teacher; they *may* be encouraged to work independently and think more creatively. Working-class kids come to school with less social capital; that is, their parents have fewer resources (linguistic consonance, social rules, and time) to assist their kids. The teacher pushes these children to fit into classroom routines and engages less frequently in substantive discourse or complex instructional tasks. Despite the modern school's rhetorical claim to eliminate ascriptive determinants of status and success, teachers' practices may help reproduce class differences.

In the Third World, all children in mass schools may be treated like working-class kids of North America. An ethnographic study of classrooms in Botswana, reveals a startling picture of children sitting passively while the teacher talks at them, asking occasionally for a choral response from the entire class to a close-ended question. Researchers Robert Prophet and Patricia Rowell focused specifically on instruction of science over a two-month period of observation. Children were not encouraged to conceptualize certain processes, say the reproduction of plants and flowers. Instead, the teacher insisted that pupils utter the correct technical terms in English. Prophet and Rowell concluded that precise elite codes were being taught, including the teacher's modern authority to relay these facts and vocabulary. Pupils had no chance to think through underlying processes or apply this knowledge to their own, usually rural, conditions.[13]

A subsequent round of observations within 150 different Botswana classrooms found significant teacher variation but revealed the same general pattern uncovered by Prophet and Rowell. Teachers were standing before the full class in 69 percent of the snapshots, lecturing at the children. Choral recitation of simple factual questions was common. Three fourths of all teacher questions (to the entire class or an individual child) had just one correct answer. In only one out of four observation periods, did a pupil vocalize a question. The government and international agencies have invested heavily in textbooks and basic instructional tools. In this Botswana study, textbooks were being employed in just 12 percent of all snapshots.[14]

Putting together these basic lessons from classroom-observation studies, a more fundamental point arises: The teacher, concerned with maintaining order among many children, must move toward bureaucratic forms of control—lecturing the class as one uniform batch of kids, spending time on administrative procedures, and assigning seat-work to silent, isolated individual pupils. Little evidence suggests that central state actors are directly manipulating teachers to engage in such bureaucratic, factory-like actions. *Yet the state, in a less obtrusive manner, is creating and legitimating the mass conditions under which socialization unfolds in the classroom.* This is particularly true within Third World political structures, comprised of elites anxious to build schools as a signal of mass participation and economic opportunity. Their emphasis is on rapid expansion of the mass school.

Education ministries may earnestly wish that teachers would engage pupils in more effective ways. But the fragile state's constraints are simply too strong, preventing central actors from moving with any precision. Political actors and education bureaucrats may urge ideological covergence on several fronts: designing and enforcing a clearer, more uniform curriculum, boosting the technical validity of national exams, circulating standard textbooks, and strengthening in-service teacher training. But often the central state simply lacks the political will or administrative capacity to implement well-meaning improvements. Or the mass conditions and uncertainties facing local teachers simply swamp these precise attempts at reform. Given the fragile state's preoccupation with signaling mass opportunity, via school expansion, political actors are quite effective in reproducing mass conditions within the local school and classroom.

The Third World state *is* often effective in allocating high status to teachers and inculcating popular expectations about what local teachers must deliver. But day to day, the teacher must set bureaucratic social rules if order, authority, and modern symbols are to be reinforced in overcrowded classrooms. In addition, the state authors a modern curriculum that is often foreign to indigenous forms of knowledge and which is broken into small, uniform pieces. The curriculum's fragmented and prescribed character fits nicely with bureaucratic social rules and practices. Much of this action is ritualistic, as John W. Meyer would emphasize. Teachers spend class time arranging lessons, talking at the pupil masses, and watching over students working on routine seat-work. Whether these teaching practices effectively impart literacy or higher-order cognitive skills is a question rarely asked. These actions are symbolically rich in maintaining order and expressing the teacher's authority within a modern, mass organization—the classroom. The teacher is acting out the behaviors and rules that are expected, and is following legitimate images of what is supposed to occur in the classroom.

Here teacher and pupil actions both demonstrate active membership in the school institution, independent of any material or cognitive effects. The state sets mass conditions that allow easy symbolic expression of membership—a prerequisite for realizing "opportunity"—while begging the question of whether much is actually being learned.

The State: Materially Poor but Symbolically Rich

Picturing the state as a well-tuned, centralized organization, vis-a-vis the school, provides many false images. Especially in the Third World, political elites often lack cohesion, the school institution often has sharp boundaries and mass support of its own, and the human processes of teaching and learning are sufficiently complex (or sacred) as to render ineffective many rational-administrative controls. Here again, I agree with Claus Offe that the state is a complicated mosaic of competing ideals, symbols, and administrative mechanisms—a structure up for grabs that is not consistently controlled by particular elites.[15] Faced with a bifurcated class structure, an artifact of colonial administration, leaders of fragile states argue that expansion of mass schooling will broaden membership in the polity and open up economic opportunity to all.

Third World states—eager to integrate balkanized tribes into one mass polity—are flowing over with contradictory signals. Political actors, for instance, argue that individuals must detach themselves from tribal collectives and customs. Instead they must become independent and self-reliant within markets and a meritocratic polity. Particularistic differences are to be tolerated, especially in early eras of nation-building when the central state is a fragile network of provincial interest groups. But all individuals are to become rational partners with the state—the universal organization that protects "autonomous" action of the individual. So education ministries preach the ideal of "developing" the individual child, romantic educational philosophy is taught in teacher training colleges, and governments create massive examination systems to carefully define each child's status. Yet mass conditions created by the state—led by political actors obsessed with using the school as a symbol of mass opportunity—discourage seeing each child as an individual. Each child is simply a part of the batch of fifty to ninety children sitting before the teacher.

In this way, the fragile state is excessively rich in symbolic currency. But mixed signals are sent down to Third World headmasters and teachers. Teachers are faced with the competing ideals of individual development versus a universal form of socialization. Teachers also are faced with enormous uncertainties created by the scarcity of instructional materials and the overwhelming abundance of kids. Quite rationally, the teacher attempts to instruct children in ways that maintain control: lecturing at the entire batch of children, routinizing simple exercises, and drawing on state-provided textbooks that chunk knowledge into discrete, predictable lessons. The teacher may attach meanings of "individual development" or "proper socialization" to their own actions. In this way, the grab-bag of contradictory symbols and meanings sent down from the state provides alternative ideals from which teachers can draw to legitimate what they do in the classroom.

State-defined Opportunity and Mass Conditions

Among this flurry of signals and chaotic administration by the state, one message stands out: The Western school is one instrument by which the family and child can get closer to modernity. The state gains support by promising (and occasionally delivering) economic growth. Material expansion allegedly leads to mass opportunity to enter the cash economy and to gain access to modern symbols (acquisition of the high-status national language, membership in bureaucratic organizations, and

109

greater proximity to modern customs). This bundle of symbols is signaled through the construction of more schools and through visible efforts to deepen the school's effects ("improving quality").

The state's crisp institutional signal of "opportunity" sparks dramatic increases in enrollment. Third World states then find that resources are insufficient to hire more teachers or to buy simple instructional materials—that is, to provide the minimum level of quality necessary for teaching even basic literacy. So again, we see pressure on the teacher to devise social rules that effectively control a burgeoning number of pupils in the classroom. And again, the teacher typically relies on bureaucratic forms of organizing: treating all children uniformly, relying on routinized lessons, and highlighting one's own authority when pupils show disinterest. The state also reinforces this standardization by distributing textbooks with uniform knowledge and facts presented in predictable lessons. But this strategy for classroom peace is more strongly rooted in the school's own desire for legitimacy and rituals which reinforce the teacher's authority, than in clear signals or administrative controls exercised by a finely-tuned state.

Importantly, these bureaucratic social rules are *not* directly handed down, or managed, by state elites. Instead, they represent the teacher's method of adapting to the mass conditions implicitly set for the school by the state.

Teacher Action in African Classrooms

The teacher can be seen as an actor who actively expresses the central state's agenda, through the official curriculum, language, and moral lessons sanctioned by political elites. Or the teacher can be seen as embedded within a bounded, autonomous school institution—though surrounded by mass conditions in crowded classrooms which flow from the central state's earnest desire to provide mass opportunity and membership in the polity. Next I report on whether the beliefs and actions of teachers reflect a close connection with the central state, or whether teachers' actions are linked more to the independent culture and commitments of the school. Evidence on this overriding question comes from school-level research conducted in Malawi over a two-year period, including both classroom observations and a teacher survey. This is the research introduced in Chapter 3.[16]

Tight correspondence between the state's educational agenda and observed teacher action might be observed within the following three domains (outlined in Figure 4.1):

School boundaries. Do teachers' ideals regarding socialization of children, the curriculum, and social rules match or diverge from modern beliefs held by political elites? Or faced with contradictory signals and constrained resources from the state, does the teacher express rituals of authority and pedagogical practices that are embedded in the school's own culture?

Classroom rules. Do explicit classroom rules, set by the teacher, reflect the state's desire to deliver a standard curriculum and to deepen the school's effect on children? Or do the teacher's rules stem from the mass conditions found in many classrooms.

Moral order. What are the implicit social rules and symbols "taught" by the teacher; in particular, what comprises legitimate forms of work, knowledge, and belief within the classroom organization? Is this moral order set by state action, the teacher's own beliefs, or the imperatives of mass conditions and the school's reactive desire for control and legitimacy.

Running across these three domains is the question of whether local teachers and pupils respond with indifference, confusion, or outright resistance. When either teachers or pupils do not conform to the state's interventions, how do authorities respond in attempting to deepen the school's effect? This sets the stage upon which Hegel's dialectic is played out: political elites are anxious to break down local differences and substitute an official public order—built on a common language, universal faith in reason and Western technical knowledge, rationalized economic systems, and bureaucratic forms of socialization and social welfare. But rather than focusing on the state's earnest desires, we must also recognize the confused and indifferent response of many teachers (and pupils). This sets in motion a dynamic that prompts further action by the state and modification of its administrative and symbolic efforts to deepen the school.

State Penetration of the School's Boundaries

Administrative Rituals[17]

State regulation of teacher action is often not very subtle within Malawi. Each teacher is expected to speak in English, or in the dominant tribe's language, after grade 4, to move through three textbooks page by page, to write down a lesson plan for each day's activities, and to hand this book over for inspection whenever requested by the headmaster (this is termed a "modern educational reform"). But the lack of subtlety I discovered that cool morning I sat in the back of a damp classroom outside Lilongwe was still surprising. Instructing grade 7 civics, the teacher was eliciting choral responses as pupils looked at a list written on the blackboard. He began with the question—

> *T:* "How does government get money?"
>
> *Ps* (in unison): "Income tax, customs duties . . ."

Then, he asked individual children:

> *T:* "What is the work of police?"
>
> *P1:* "To arrest kids."
>
> *P2:* "To protect houses."

Getting the attention of the class, the teacher (through his intonation) then elicited everyone to repeat what he said:

> *T:* "The police work to maintain peace and order."
>
> *Ps* (in unison): "To maintain peace and order."

The teacher then called on individual pupils to recite the six types of police in Malawi (as he wrote each type on the blackboard). Then reviewing each branch, he continued:

> *T:* "If the PMF police came here, what will (*sic*) they do?"
>
> *P3:* "They will deal with a riot or a strike."
>
> *T:* "Now the special branch . . . when you go to public meetings and see well-dressed men, they are checking on whether the situation is okay. If it is not, they take away the leaders."
>
> My note: of the forty-seven pupils in the room, about ten are visibly fading from the conversation. The teacher then erases the six types of police, proceeding to call on individual pupils asking the functions of each type. This

serves to get the attention of previously disinterested youngsters.

The education ministry can not afford to write and publish a civics textbook for primary school pupils. Only in the past decade have texts become available for arithmetic, English, and Chichewa. But this factual material on police was pulled from a modest secondary school text which serves as this primary teacher's curriculum guide.[18]

Political elites within the Malawian state often do penetrate the school's boundaries through administrative practices. The state's emphasis on modern bureaucratic management and Western social ideals can be seen in the action and artifacts of most school headmasters. But does this penetration from the center result in material change at the school level, touching the roles and behaviors enacted by local actors? Or do headmasters and teachers simply comply symbolically with government directives, insulating their pre-existing roles and daily routines?

Take, for instance, the action of Malawi's twenty-two district education officers—mid-level bureaucrats who link the central ministry with every school headmaster. These officers not only distribute teachers' salaries each month, they also try to sharpen management and improve the school's moral order. At a school in the capital city, one headmaster had posted "administrative tips" sent out by the district education officer. This circular called for "radical improvements" in eleven specific areas, including:

1. Punctuality. Make sure that both teachers and pupils are punctual so that lessons start promptly and that there is no time wasted. . . .

3. Prolonged Break Periods. Avoid spending more time outside the classroom after break periods are over. Remember that time is money.

4. Thorough Lesson Preparations. Lesson planning be done (*sic*) for all subjects to be taught each day. . . .

6. Pupils' Discipline. Intensify pupils' discipline inorder (*sic*) to create and maintain favourable conditions for teaching and learning . . . It is our responsibility to mould the child.

9. Pupils Cleanliness. Wearing of school Uniform be encouraged (*sic*) so that pupils are smartly dressed and should look clean.

113

The circular closes with the bold declaration, "PLEASE ALWAYS REMEMBER TO READ THE HANDBOOK ON PRIMARY SCHOOL ADMINISTRATION WHICH IS IN YOUR POSSESSION."

When a naive researcher asks headmasters or teachers whether lesson plans are actually written, a curious look is appropriated, then in a rush three or four booklets are produced containing past and present lesson plans. These booklets vary in their specificity. Yet most indicate, for each class period, what steps were planned, how the lesson was actually carried out, and how pupils handled the material. The teacher may specify actual vocabulary words presented or references to pages covered from a textbook. Within the neighborhood of Kawale, one teacher dutifully indicated that a "political song" (*Popanda a Ngwazi likulu ku Lilongwe*) was taught on March 27. The next day this grade 8 teacher presented a "religious song" ("He Rolled by the Water"). She commented that while most pupils liked the political song (in Chichewa), many could not master the gospel hymm's lyrics (in English).

In their modest offices headmasters usually post elaborate schedules showing what subjects each teacher is presenting each period. Nation-wide subjects are divided neatly into these 35 minute segments from grade 1 on, including language, math, music, geography, agriculture, and religion (that is, Scottish Presbyterian thought, stemming from the dominant missionaries under British rule). Quite often headmasters will post the fee collection schedule and deadlines, reminding teachers to speak to pupils that have yet to pay.

The fragile state, attempting to implement a modern bureaucratic form of organization, speaks to school headmasters. Despite infrequent direct regulation by state inspectors or district officers (on average, once every 2 years), most headmasters proceed with at least the symbols of rational administration: routinizing the teacher's actions through lesson plans, arranging simple bits of knowledge into thirty-five-minute segments, and admonishing teachers to transmit Western signals of virtue and character (Western-style uniforms, promptness, and cleanliness). Even in the face of weak and infrequent sanctions, compliance with the state's agenda is common—even in remote rural schools far from any paved road. The state implicitly labels these demands as "modern rules" which will presumably deepen the school's effect on children.

More materially, bureaucratic forms of control reduce uncertainty in the eyes of local headmasters and teachers. Primary schools in Malawi can have up to 2,500 pupils attending; Standard 1 teachers commonly have seventy children sitting in their classrooms each morning. The meanings of order and discipline, attached by the state to rationalized administrative action, signal that local actors hold the authority and means for reducing uncertainty within the mass school. No one asks whether such practices boost pupil achievement; they are simply seen as basic forms of organization, necessary for boosting the school's legitimacy and the teacher's authority.

When the state employs bureaucratic means for reducing uncertainty at the school level, these rules often are passed on by the headmaster to shape the teacher's beliefs and behavior. Teachers may come to feel little professional autonomy or control over their work, especially in the Third World, as revealed by recent studies of teaching in Nigeria and Thailand. Lorin Anderson and his colleagues found, for instance, that only 10 percent of teachers interviewed in each country believed that they had full control over topics presented in their classrooms. Only slightly more teachers felt they could even control "classroom organization." Fewer teachers perceived control over student promotion requirements.[19] Thus classic bureaucratic controls which link the strong central state and local headmasters are simply passed on: headmasters, mimicking the form of control to which they are subjected, attempt to rationally control and homogenize the behavior of their teachers.

Competing Clubs: Limits to the State's Penetration

Are these pressures by the state and headmaster sufficiently strong to consistently shape the teacher's action and beliefs inside the classroom? I have shown how political elites—with clear intent or through inadvertent mimicry of modern organizing—shape the social rules and knowledge that are transmitted into the classroom. Yet how does the teacher respond to this pressure to construct bureaucratic social rules and to express modern symbols? I see three basic factors that limit the state's actual influence over the classroom teacher.

First, *the state's capacity to provide material resources is constrained*, which eats into the state's own authority. Despite limited resources, Third World governments have been very effective in constructing school buildings, often collaborating with traditional local leaders and drawing on villagers' eagerness to build even simple structures. But the second injection of resources, necessary for deepening the school's effect on children's achievement, either never comes or is very modest. In most Third World countries teachers remain in short supply. Our Malawi school survey found an average of 119 pupils enrolled in grade 1 classes (with about eighty-five attending each day); attendance falls to about forty-five pupils per classroom by grade 6. Most primary school teachers in this African nation have not completed secondary school (as reviewed in Chapter 3). Many come from families that are still engaged in subsistence farming. Almost two thirds of the teachers we surveyed had no desks for pupils in their classrooms. Over half the teachers received fewer than ten textbooks for their entire class each year. With this questionable level of teacher quality and extreme shortage of instructional materials, should we expect the state, via the school, to have much impact on children's learning?

On the other hand, the scarcity of instructional material may inadvertently strengthen the state's authority over what legitimate knowledge is presented to pupils. In the Third World, teachers must rely heavily on state-written textbooks, since this is often the only written material or pedagogical "technology" available. The situation in Malawi is shared by Nigeria and Thailand, as revealed by the recent research. Most teachers report the use of texts in organizing their lessons. But in Nigeria, less than 10 percent of teachers reported use of pupil workbooks (blank sheets of paper stapled together). In both countries, even routinized instructional materials, such as worksheets containing exercises, were rarely available. Books other than texts are rarely found in African classrooms; libraries in primary schools are non-existent. The central state's influence—in casting official knowledge and communicating modern symbols via textbooks—goes unchallenged.

Importantly, the patterning of headmaster and teacher behavior occurs with little regulation from above. Teachers reported that their headmasters visited their classroom just two times over the prior three years to evaluate their performances. Headmasters reported that school inspectors drop by just once a year, usually to check on *signals* of rational organization: the presence of a class schedule, records of school fees collected, an inventory of textbooks, a check to see whether teachers actually showed up that day, and an assessment of how tidy the school grounds appear to be. Similarly, teachers submit their detailed lesson plans to the headmaster (listing "goals, content, and effectiveness"); but headmasters rarely observe teachers and provide substantive advice on teaching methods. The latter process is too complex to mesh with the state's "efficient" check of symbols that represent a tight school structure.

Second, the state's influence on teachers is constrained by the *incon-*

sistent character of ideological messages emanating from political elites. This is especially true as fragile (or stumbling) states struggle to rapidly build (or reinforce) institutions that will incorporate diverse groups. A Third World government's attempt at bureaucratic control, for example, is constrained by contradictions inherent within Western views of the state and broader polity: (a) The modern state defines the individual as a rational creature who can be "developed"; but fledgling secular states must focus on nation-building through the incorporation of balkanized tribes into bureaucratic work and social institutions. (b) The Western state is supposed to tolerate particular features of local communities; but it also pushes uniform faith in rational forms of knowledge and symbols, including sanctification of reason, science, and individualistic manifestations of choice. (c) The state, dominated by elites, must aid the accumulation of capital and draw on a flexible labor force to support parallel faith in economic expansion; but political agencies must also redistribute wealth and broaden symbolic forms of "opportunity" to construct and reinforce its own popular legitimacy. (d) Opportunity and modern progress can be more cheaply portrayed in symbolic forms than in material terms. Schools, for instance, can teach high-status languages, talk about math and science, and rhetorically link schooling to higher paying jobs. Of course, *signaling opportunity* to enter the modern world does not guarantee material gains for the masses. Where schooling expands more quickly than jobs in the cash economy, political elites must contend with disenchanted youths and parents. And if the state moves too quickly, ignoring tribal traditions and forms of authority, secular elites lose legitimacy.

The fragile state's tendency to emit mixed messages was crisply illustrated one day as I observed two energetic teachers in a southern Malawi primary school, close to the Mozambique border. Walking into the grade 4 classroom, I noticed that the day's attendance was written on the blackboard: "48 girls and 52 boys." A science teacher accompanied the regular teacher in presenting a talk on different types of soil. In large urban schools—this primary had over two thousand pupils attending each day—it is common to see a teacher with specific training in mathematics or science. The fact that a specialist joins the regular teacher adds to the status of the subject. And this specialist came with some hands-on material: canisters filled with five different types of dirt. In rapid succession, the two teachers gave each pair of children a dash of brown soil, red soil, sandy soil, and rain soil. The science teacher pursued tangents on how to read a rain gauge and on which soils would support more crops. The science teacher talked at this batch of one hundred pupils, eliciting choral pronunciation of terms in English: "milliliter," "this is clay soil," "rocks lay beneath this kind of soil."

The content of this lesson was quite relevant, especially to children who spent part of each day working on the family plot. Yet the pieces of knowledge (facts) were simply spoken at this densely packed group of children. This was science—a high-status topic that required a special authority to explain the topic in English. This modern set of codes was delivered within a mass setting. Dishing out dirt to one hundred kids must be done quickly; information is attached to each pile; children repeat these fragments of knowledge; the teacher moves on quickly to the next chunk of information. Marking the class period's end, the teacher ordered everyone to engage in quick calisthenics, "Stand up! . . . hands up, forward, side, sit down." All one hundred obediently responded, although several had to lift their drowsy heads off their desks before popping up. The science specialist lauched into the next topic: "germs and pests that live in dirty houses."

Teachers' Ideologies

When we examine teachers' own beliefs about schooling and socialization the third constraint on the state's local penetration arises. *Teachers' own beliefs and behaviors vary*, spawned either within the school's own institutional boundaries or determined by the state's mixed messages.

Our interviews of teachers in Malawi included questions regarding their beliefs and actions within classrooms. Teachers commonly face the dilemma of whether they should socialize children to fit into the school regimen and later into "the adult world." Or should a romantic and individualistic view be taken, emphasizing liberation of each child from dominant structures and pursuit of the child's own curiosities. Bronwyn Davies, working in Australia, reports on this quandry facing teachers.[20] Of course, this mirrors, and returns us to, the contradiction facing the secular state: to encourage individual autonomy and tolerance of particularistic differences *or* to pursue hegemonic faith in a homogenized nation and bureaucratic forms of organization.

As we have seen, Rousseau and Durkheim argued that only a strong legitimate state could protect individual autonomy. Marx attacked Hegel on whether a centralized state would act in the interests of the broader polity. Talcott Parsons argued that schools would never truly "educate" the individual child; to do so would only destabilize the cultural foundations of the polity and the state.[21] We were curious as to whether this contradiction within the state was reflected in the signals expressed by teachers in this southern African context.

Our initial findings on the educational ideologies of teachers in Malawi, as well as their perceptions of their classroom behavior are quite interesting. We asked teachers, for instance, about the importance they place on three possible goals of schooling. Seventy percent of the teachers reported that improving "pupils' ways of thinking" is a very important goal. Just 47 percent believed that assistance in getting a better job is very important. We also asked about more specific teaching practices related to how children should be socialized. Fifty-one percent said that they "strongly agreed" with the statement: "schools should teach children rules and how to fit into society." Fewer (38 percent) strongly agreed that "pupils learn more when they listen and ask fewer questions." But only 19 percent strongly agreed that "school should teach children how to pursue their own individual goals and interests." The greatest consensus was on a statement that fell between a liberal-individualistic versus a strong fitting-in view of socialization. Sixty percent of all teachers strongly agreed that "school should teach children to cooperate and respect other people." In short, ideologies held by the typical teacher are not clear-cut, often reflecting a mix of educational philosophy.

Mass Conditions and the Teacher's Pursuit of Authority

Romantic or functionalist beliefs are one thing. But when the teacher actually is faced with sixty or seventy children in the classroom, how does he or she structure action? Reports by teachers of what they do are not always reliable. Teachers' perceptions in Malawi, however, closely matched the observational findings from other work, including the recent studies in Nigeria and Thailand, and my ongoing work in Botswana (with Wes Snyder and David Chapman).

Teachers in Malawi report spending 45 percent of their class time lecturing and interacting with the entire class (including presentation of material, reading aloud from textbooks, asking for choral recitations, and asking questions of individual pupils while the class listens). Thirty percent of teachers' time was reportedly spent supervising pupils working silently on exercises (in Malawi, usually writing out arithmetic problems or short vocabulary lists in their exercise books). These teacher actions commonly occur in a thirty-five-minute sequence like that which I observed in a four-room school close to Lunzu:

- The fourth-grade teacher begins the period by writing a multiplication problem on the board (.252 kilograms times 3). (Note: since this is math, the teacher shifts to speaking English.)
- The teacher asks for a choral response (from all seventy-two pupils) to each calculation: "3 times 2 is? . . . 3 times 5 is? . . ." Whenever the response is not loud and crisp, the teacher speaks more sharply, "3 times 2 is what?!"
- After working through three such problems with the entire class, the teacher writes another problem on the board and directs all pupils to calculate it in their exercise books. (Note: all pupils have an exercise book and a pencil.)
- As pupils finish the problem they eagerly wave their books, remaining seated on the cold concrete floor. One by one the teacher circulates to each pupil, checking answers. Getting to seventy-two pupils requires only 20 minutes. (Note: pupil attention drifts as the teacher continues to circulate.)
- The teacher then goes back to the blackboard, asking individual pupils to stand and work through the problem. When a pupil makes a mistake, the teacher quickly interrupts and moves to another pupil, many of whom are emphatically waving their hands and snapping their fingers. Those pupils who made a mistake, four in all, remain standing until a correct answer is given.

This sequence of talking at the entire class, eliciting choral responses, then assigning an individually-performed exercise is quite common, regardless of the subject being taught. The important point here is that the *conditions of mass schooling* drive teacher action, not the more complex and diverse ideologies that teachers hold in their heads. This pedagogical sequence aims at keeping the attention of the entire class and demanding that each child work alone on an exercise (at least for a very brief time). Below, I explore the unquestioned moral order and explicit social rules reinforced within such a structure.

Here I want to stress two parallel points. First, teachers hold conflicting and mixed beliefs about socialization, a contradiction rooted in the ideologies of the modern state. Even if a teacher wants to attend to the individual curiousities of a student or encourage cooperative action by pupils, it is very difficult. Faced with so many pupils, scarce instructional resources, and a centrally prescribed curriculum—conditions set by the modern state—the teacher simply (and rationally) seeks to control and energize these crowded, restless children. Second, the Western state commonly sends out mixed ideological signals to those charged with formally socializing children. But the state's preoccupation with the symbols of mass opportunity lead to concrete classroom conditions that necessitate mass bureaucratic ways of organizing kids and routinized presentation of "facts."

School as Church: Reinforcing Teacher Authority

The state, attempting to shape teachers and pedagogical practices, is at times stymied by the school institution's own entrenched culture. *The school is an organization, at times distinct from the state, that has constructed its own forms of authority, rituals of membership, and signals of status.*

Philip Cusick, during his ethnographic study of a North American high school, found two different organizations actually operating within the mass school. The "production system" involves the official technical agenda of the school, including instruction, the explicit curriculum, and testing. But this organization is supported by the "maintenance system," that is, by the authority and social rules required to maintain order within the classroom. In a more subtle form, headmasters and teachers are concerned with establishing and reinforcing the child's membership within the school organization, independent of his or her actual technical achievement. The teacher, anxious to strengthen the child's loyalty to the school and to maintain order in the classroom, draws on institutionalized forms of authority. So teachers follow the role behaviors that are expected of them as "modern teachers." As John W. Meyer points out, most teachers worldwide lecture at large batches of children, not because it is effective but because this is what teachers are expected to do. The teacher's authority is rooted in following such scripts that award legitimacy and meaning to their actions. So, in Malawi some teachers sharply reprimand children who fail to buy or wear bright blue uniforms to school—not because this boosts achievement but because it signals membership in the government school and reverence for the teacher's own authority.[22]

Sounds of Clashing Symbols

Under the fragile state, the teacher is the arbiter between central elites seeking uniform socialization and plural tribes which resist or ignore this pursuit of hegemony. In attending to the classroom's "maintenance system" the teacher must accommodate these local differences. To build cohesion teachers must depart from the central state's socialization agenda. For instance, teachers in Malawi are expected to teach all subjects in English after grade 4. In addition, the language spoken by the dominant tribe—which controls the national government—is taught beginning in the first grade. Once you leave the towns and the central region dominated by the Chewa tribe, few children will understand Chichewa or English. So teachers commonly speak in Yao, Tumbuka, or one of the other thirty-five tribal languages spoken. Instruction in English holds enormous status among the political elite; but the teacher must obviously speak in the children's tribal language if any cameraderie is to be built inside the classroom.

In remote rural schools, headmasters are apologetic that Chichewa and English are not spoken by their teachers. These schools enroll children of subsistence farmers, living in sparsely populated villages often a day's walk from the nearest paved road. The only government official they see is the district education officer, once a month when he brings teachers' salaries in cash. If teachers pressed the language of a foreign tribe (be it the language of Chewa political elites or of British economic elites), children would understand little and the school would alienate parents. In this case the central government would be seen as too ideological and irrelevant. But by delivering subjects in the indigenous language, the state's socialization agenda appears less obtrusive.[23]

At times, even the state will attempt to accommodate local forms of authority within textbooks and the curriculum. Early one morning we arrived at a primary school close to rural Dowa. The rains had come two weeks prior. The morning air was cool and damp. Entering the dark, stark classroom I saw just eleven youngsters, all sitting on the floor, which my butt soon told me was cold and wet. Embarrassed, the teacher flew out the door, returning with an old chair . . . a scarce but strong symbol of respect for his strange white visitor. The teacher continued reading a passage from the government's grade 7 English textbook ". . . Mkandawire, the local headman, sat talking to his fellow villagers. The rains had not come that season, and the villagers were worried about their crops and the health of their children. The headman had thought much about why the rain had not come. He was presenting possible explanations. . . ."

Interestingly, the story goes on to present several spiritual and traditional explanations for why the rains had not come. After reading the story, the teacher asked pupils questions in English, practicing their reading comprehension. But the traditional wisdom of village headmen continued to receive respect throughout the discussion. This section of the textbook provides a collection of traditional stories, at times blended with Western knowledge and symbols. One historical story deals with a woman who allegedly fools slave traders by pretending she's a witch. Another tells of a middle class man who uses a clock to make sure he catches his bus on time, and features pictures of him jumping from bed dressed in pajamas running to the bus stop. Very few Malawians can afford to ride a bus, and fewer sleep in beds. Pajamas are seen as an incredibly funny artifact worn only by the British.[24]

Many teachers are quite active within their classrooms. The life and pace of interaction between these teachers and their many pupils is remarkable. Their common lesson sequence does engage the majority of pupils: presenting a chunk of material, eliciting choral responses, assigning short twenty-minute exercises, then reviewing the material by working out the problems on the blackboard. The resulting cohesion maintains the teacher's authority and sanctions the discrete bits of information contained within the official curriculum. This routine also allows the teacher to demonstrate to the headmaster, in a standardized way, how far the class has progressed in the textbook. Whether this regimen effectively imparts literacy or useful social skills is rarely asked. The teacher's legitimacy is simply reinforced by following institutionalized rules for how he or she is supposed to act. There is ample faith that these actions will lead to desired socialization and academic outcomes.

Occasionally Malawian teachers set down social rules that contradict the otherwise mass structure of the classroom. Maintaining order and discipline remains a concern. Yet the teacher relinquishes control, encouraging pupils to engage in more complex individual activities or to work cooperatively in groups. This combination of high energy, engagement, and more lateral interaction among children was illustrated by the following sequence observed in one classroom not far from the capital city of Lilongwe:

—The teacher begins the Chichewa period (grade 3) by passing out textbooks. Few pupils own their own. I noted that on the blackboard was written, "67 on roll, 59 present." The teacher commanded all children to stand and touch their toes, raise their arms over their heads, and clap their hands. The morning is warm, but the children seem keen on getting off the concrete floor for a few moments. These sudden calisthenics signal the beginning of the next thirty-five-minute period.

—The teacher writes twelve Chichewa words on the board and begins pointing to each word. This prompts a wild waving of hands and snapping of fingers—a stylized snapping that results from a sharp simultaneous flicking of the wrist and fingers. Performed by this batch of kids, it sounds like a muffled orchestra of crickets. (I think to myself that Victorian missionary teachers would have been shocked to witness this audible African sign of eagerness in the classroom.)

—A five-sentence paragraph containing these new words is read by the teacher from the Chichewa text. She then bangs an aluminum pot with a broad stick . . . like a metal drum. This sends the children scurrying around, forming into familiar groups of three or four. As the dust (literally) settles, one child in each group begins reading the passage out loud to the other group members. The teacher circles around the class, listening to recitations within each group, for about 15 minutes.

—The teacher grabs the pot and stick once more; the same piercing percussion sends pupils back into their tidy columns, as if they were sitting one behind each other in desks (but in this classroom there are no desks).

—Again, the pupils are told to stand and run through their well-learned exercises. This round includes turning in circles, jumping up and down, pointing to the blackboard, the door,

and the windows (where no glass remains). The names of
these classroom features are shouted out in English.
—The teacher then reads ten Chichewa words which pupils
write in their exercise books. They exchange books to read
how their partner wrote the words. The teacher again
circulates around to all fifty-nine, checking their spelling.

I recall my initial fright in seeing the instinctive compliance exhibited
by these small children, quickly replying to the teacher's every com-
mand. But within the routine, children were encouraged to interact with
each other. First, reading to each other. Later, reading their partner's
written Chichewa words. The content and form of this cooperative action
was certainly prescribed by the teacher. But this horizontal interaction
between small groups or pairs of children departed strongly from the
usual pattern where the teacher constantly interacts with the entire mass
of pupils, or where pupils work in isolation from one another.

Classroom Rules and the Moral Order

Thus far I have focused on the state's efficacy in shaping the curriculum and social rules upon which Malawian teachers come to rely.
Second, I have emphasized how the state inadvertently sets mass classroom conditions, leading teachers to become obsessed with maintaining
control and reinforcing their own authority. We have explored how the
state's intentional actions are undercut by mixed ideological symbols
and by the teacher's necessary accommodation with local cultures.

The state, especially in the Third World, touches the classroom in a
third way: by legitimating the teacher's role in providing moral lessons
to children. Durkheim argued that all tribes (including modern secular
ones) hold certain ideals and rules as sacred, unquestioned commitments
or forms of behavior. Robert Dreeben's argument (as detailed in Chapter
2) becomes important again in this context: the school implicitly attempts
to teach children to achieve in an individualistic, competitive manner.
In the Anglo-Protestant context, working together is either labelled as
cheating, or is seen as a low-status way of proving one's merit. This
implicit form of socialization, operating beneath the explicit curriculum,
helps reproduce the sacred cultural commitment to individualism and
competition found in Western tribes. Durkheim goes further to show

that tribes develop elaborate rituals for symbolically expressing sacred commitments. Symbolic expressions may hold little technical effect on achievement, but they allow members a chance to display their solidarity with important ideological commitments. As Basil Bernstein suggests, the function of ritual is "to relate the individual to a social order, to heighten respect for that order, to revivify that order within the individual and, in particular, to deepen acceptance of the procedures which are used to maintain continuity, order and boundary."[25] Let's look at the rituals found in African classrooms that serve to reinforce the teacher's authority and control, as well as enable pupils to express their membership in the classroom structure.

The Teacher's Strong Authority

Most African teachers are members of the small class of people who are literate and who receive a steady wage in cash. The teacher also holds the power to allocate forms of secular merit and virtue to children. Relatively few children persist through primary school and enter secondary school. But those that do persist gain a shot at entering the modern economic sector to make a steady wage. This institutionalized role as gate-keeper, legitimated by the state, brings enormous status to the teacher. Yet day to day in the classroom, many teachers feel that they must demonstrate their strict authority. This is particularly true in settings like Malawi, where colonial schools historically reflected deference to authoritarian officialdom, and the overcrowded conditions of mass schooling create uncertainty for which tight control appears to be an effective antidote.

Whenever a Malawian pupil must urinate, he or she is required to seek out the teacher, who is usually standing at the front of the class. Before all, the pupil bows down onto one knee, folds his or her hands, and requests a leave. Two or three children during each class period will typically go through this rather fluid motion, with little apparent embarrassment. But as a ritual, signaling control over the child's most basic movements, the exercise is significant.

Often when a thirty-five-minute class period has been completed, the teacher will signal to a pupil to pick up a rag and erase the blackboard, as the teacher moves to the back of the classroom. The teacher will just stand, scanning over the pupils, until the blackboard is spotless. This crisply signals the shift to a new subject, as well as the teacher's authority to assign a routine chore while he or she simply waits. Similarly, when the headmaster or a visitor enters the classroom, the teacher bows and clasps one wrist as they shake hands. The teacher is thereby displaying his or her deference to persons that are higher in the status order. I have often thought about how pupils, who are subordinated daily to the teacher's authority, view their own teacher's self-subordination to the headmaster or the occasional government representative.

These rituals reinforce the hierarchical form of authority found in the "modern" African school. In fact, the severe asymmetry of authority found in Malawian schools suggests that Dreeben's emphasis on achievement and individualism may not apply in many Third World settings. The modern state may preach the virtues of self-reliance, higher productivity, and entrepreneurial initiative. But the structure of authority and status previously found in colonial schools (be they operated by imperial administrations or by missions) continues to be reproduced. Here the liberal, romantic side of the Western state can not be operationalized in the face of classrooms spilling over with children. Note again, the *post-colonial* state is attempting to broaden opportunity to achieve higher status and higher income by opening access to the school institution. But the mass conditions and uncertainty which result inside the classroom push the teacher to seek control, and to engage in rituals that signal authority but which do very little to encourage learning.

Corporate Forms of Merit and Virtue

Following Dreeben's line, the classroom's moral order should be marked by two other sacred rules . . . each pupil's level of achievement and merit are judged along *universal* and *highly specific criteria.* Following classic bureaucratic mores (a la Max Weber), the teacher does not use personalized or complex benchmarks for assessing each child's virtues or weaknesses. Indeed, this more personalized approach is defined as inefficient and unmodern. So within mass classroom conditions, the Third World teacher tries to look modern by evaluating pupils along the state's definition of achievement and personal virtue: mastery of the knowledge contained in a universal, routinized curriculum. Fragile states, struggling to define common commitments and sacred facts, also construct national examinations that efficiently test recall of simple facts. The teacher then moves through the text each day transmitting standardized knowledge and codes: names of famous places and geographic features, arithmetic procedures, labels and functions of government organizations, vocabulary and grammatical rules, and (in Malawi) the basic precepts of Scottish Presbyterian ideals. The child comes from a traditional form of socialization into this foreign setting called the school, takes on the label of "pupil," and is assigned to a new role that is defined by the teacher; and the pupil quickly learns that status depends on his or her capacity to absorb and recall many facts embedded within a foreign, yet somehow *modern*, structure of knowledge.

The knowledge and symbols taught are certainly "restricted" in Basil Bernstein's sense of the term. Whether the teacher is instructing on the process of multiplication or on the purposes of the national government, these "facts" are presented as pieces of information that are sacred and unquestioned. This information is to be practiced and memorized, reified as a commodity that holds status in both the school and in other modern organizations. This knowledge may not have immediate relevance to children's own lives—in contrast to their implicit socialization at home (linked to caring for other children, working on the family plot, finding fire wood, preparing meals, and learning moral codes set down by parents and village leaders). Nor are these facts and codes presented in school subject to debate or competing viewpoints. Knowledge apparently is not something to be manipulated by the learner; it is simply to be internalized and recalled in order to advance in the status system as prescribed by the school and the state. Where the state sorts youths and defines the meritocratic order around national exams, the facts contained therein instantly receive legitimacy as what should be presented in the classroom.

In much of the Third World, school-based knowledge is purposefully *subversive*. These social facts and moral codes are manifestations of modern behaviors and beliefs, implicitly stigmatizing pre-modern forms of knowledge and local authority. Only authorities found within the school, holding social power through their link with the state, can ordain children with these modern forms of knowledge and social rules. Parents can not teach modern literacy; village headmen hold no authority to teach secular morality or forms of achievement and status. Only members of the school are credible for this project.

Take, for instance, the classroom in a school far north of Mzuzu within which I had been observing. The fourth-grade teacher had just completed the science period. She began writing the following story—in English—on the blackboard:

> "The Cinema. One Saturday morning Mr. Kapezi took the four
> children to the cinema in his car. He drove for some time.
> Then they saw a big building. Is this the cinema? one child
> asked. I think so, said Mr. Kapezi, but let's ask whether the
> children's cinema is showing this morning . . ."[My note: After
> spending 15 minutes writing the story on the board, as pupils
> talk among themselves, the teacher begins asking individual
> pupils to read just one word out loud.]

T: First word?

P1: One.

T: Next?

P2: Saturday.

Only the teacher had an English textbook. So she held it up to show her seventy-three pupils the picture of the family driving up to a huge theatre building. Now the school in which this lesson occurred is located at least 70 kilometers from the nearest movie theatre. Perhaps one or two of the families represented in the classroom actually owned a car. Once the teacher got the story on the blackboard, she artfully questioned individual pupils, had some read the entire passage, asked for translations into Chichewa, and asked individual pupils to stand and take follow-up questions to ensure that they comprehended this foreign subject written in a foreign tongue. While most of these kids came from subsistence farming families and had never seen a movie theatre, they were most excited about the idea of visiting a modern cinema.

Powerful, Mystifying Civic Institutions

Schooling is subversive in another way: it legitimates a formal civic world that operates above traditional communities and the individual. The individual child is initially embedded in particularistic family and village settings. In traditional Third World settings, such as rural villages and even urban neighborhoods in Malawi, the child is not socially constructed to be an "individual" operating independently of the family collective. But once the child enters the mass school, the individual is juxtaposed to formal civic institutions which together represent modern work and social roles. So even very young children learn about agencies of the state, universal attributes and obligations of a "citizen," and knowledge and symbols linked to work and life in urban organizations. Of course, this civic world is quite different from the organization of work, family, and political authority found within traditional communities. And to make sense of this (nation-wide) civic sphere the individual child is urged to adopt behaviors and beliefs outside of the traditional community, and to judge his or her own status along benchmarks defined by modern institutions.

The Western school tries to construct an immediate link between the newly individuated child and the state. Early theorists advocating the construction of secular institutions—like Hegel and Durkheim—argued that direct and universal links with certain political ideals and agencies would help break down tribal conflict. At the same time, the modern democratic state must tolerate particularistic diversity if it is to maintain popular support and legitimacy. Thus the state demands allegiance to certain ideals and obligations (voting, taxes, military unity), but the modern state also formally defines certain attributes and entitlements of "the individual" (rationality, self-reliance, autonomy). Now if you grow up in a remote rural village in Malawi, efforts by the distant nation-state to define the individual in these terms makes no sense at all. It would be like a good Protestant in the United States looking at how faraway Rome is trying to sculpt the character and obligations of Catholics. The centralized Vatican simply holds no legitimacy. But if, through schooling, the central state gains credibility and authority, then the state's definition of the individual and one's direct connection with it begin to seem more reasonable. The authority of parents, villages, and local churches of course erodes as this larger construct of "civic institutions" gains legitimacy and becomes an accepted social fact.

Exchanging Labor for Modern Symbols

The mass school is the first formal civic institution encountered by the child. The youngster, surrounded by fifty or sixty others, must figure out how to "achieve" and gain positive evaluations from the teacher. This involves paying respect to adult authorities who are not from their village, as well as learning what's so special about languages, organizations, and behaviors exhibited in town. The individual child then comes to separate his or herself from indigenous affiliations and traditional authority. But, as we have seen, the moral order of the classroom greatly limits the individual child's discretion. That is, the child may take on a more individualistic sense of self, but achievement must occur within a classroom setting that demands engagement and conformity (or the child is stigmatized as a "failure").

Recently scholars have emphasized how this moral order reflects the state's interest in teaching children how to exchange their labor for external rewards. Pupils are encouraged to perform individually. But rewards for individually performed tasks are externally allocated by the teacher (or the state in the case of national examinations). Intrinsic rewards for learning and achieving are rarely cued or encouraged in African classrooms. Thus children learn that their labor is to be traded for symbolic rewards: test scores, grades, promotion through standardized grades, and even positive affection from friendly teachers. These rewards hold currency primarily in the school. High national exam scores and promotion into secondary school may yield economic benefits eventually; but in the short-run the high achieving pupil comes to value rewards that are legitimated inside the school organization itself.

The pupil comes to define "work" as action that yields a reward from an external agent (the teacher or headmaster) who is embedded in a formal, mass institution. If a child's own parents previously succeeded in this system and hold sufficient cultural capital to assist, then a pupil can decipher this organization. But if the child's parents left school after 2 years to work on the family plot or in the city as a street vendor, then the child may have difficulty in making sense out of this foreign-seeming process of trading labor for symbolic rewards.[26]

This line of thought and research emphasizes how labor comes to be seen as a commodity, to be freely traded for rewards defined and allocated by institutional elites. The child remains on the periphery of the school "production process" as a rather passive participant, given little opportunity to manipulate knowledge or to pursue intrinsic rewards from learning. Interestingly, Marx was not especially critical about the construction of secular organizations—only that certain classes were kept at the periphery and that labor became linked to exchange rather than to intrinsically rewarding activity.

In addition, the mass school's definition of membership in modern institutions makes assumptions about the *location* and *content* of legitimate human action (including labor). In the Third World, the conflict between village (or even the urban neighborhood) and bureaucratic arrangements of work and social life is very clear. The school lends credibility to knowledge, rules, and symbols that are located within corporate organizations—be they government or economic structures. Not only is the individual's required (exchange) orientation constructed with regard to work and reward. But the location and the content—where and with what material—of legitimate labor is implicitly socialized through the moral lessons taught in the classroom.

Summary

Do strong states breed strong teachers? Central political elites, in the African context, do penetrate the school's institutional boundaries. First, the state legitimates and enforces bureaucratic forms and rituals: telling headmasters to keep tidy class schedules, requiring teachers to punch in and punch out, demanding teachers to write out each lesson plan. Such classic routinization and breaking down seemingly complex tasks into simple behaviors signals that the school, though poor in material resources, can take on the attributes of a modern bureaucracy. Second, the state writes curricula that contain Western forms of knowledge and symbols. Third, the state sanctions a moral order in the classroom, licensing the teacher as a secular authority who holds social rules and codes that are superior to indigenous forms of authority and knowledge. Fourth, and perhaps most importantly, the state sets in place the mass conditions present in most Third World classrooms. Faced with up to ninety children, the teacher becomes preoccupied with maintaining control, engaging a dense batch of youngsters, and reinforcing his or her own authority.

The fragile state may spew rhetoric about encouraging individual, personalized development of the child. But the teacher must deliver a uniform package of facts and knowledge to all children, and evaluate each along universal and simple criteria. Individual work is encouraged, not more complex forms of cooperation (such as democratic social rules). And each child's virtue and moral worth is judged along the same secular criteria which emphasize memorization of sacred facts and bits of knowledge. The central state's macro agenda of extending mass opportunity and building a nation-wide consciousness largely defines the mass conditions facing most African teachers.

Yet characterizing the teacher as the state's messenger, as prior theorists would have it, is *not* an accurate representation. Signals coming down from the state are mixed. Does modern socialization involve training each child to fit into the state's view of knowledge, achievement, and status? Or is the state serious about individual development and tolerance of local particulars? Teachers do not lay distinctly on one end of this spectrum or the other; nor do most actors within the central state. In fact, many teachers in the plural societies of southern Africa must accommodate widely diverse local languages and forms of village authority. If they do not, the school's legitimacy is severely undercut and drop-out rates climb even higher than they already are.

In addition, the school is a bounded organization, defined by its own sacred facts, rituals, and rules of membership. Teachers may rely on lecturing at pupils, assuming that the mass of youngsters will stay engaged, and on signaling that control will be maintained. This has little to do with boosting levels of achievement; but it signals that the teacher is credible and doing what he or she is expected to do. The state—by setting mass conditions in the classroom—reinforces pedagogical rituals like lecturing at children. But occasionally a teacher will re-create classroom rules to encourage more complex cognitive tasks or cooperative action between pupils. Provided this does not undercut control and authority, the teacher can diverge from customary teaching practices.

The state *unknowingly* determines the mass conditions found in African classrooms. Then, faced with ineffective schools and teachers, political elites mount fresh strategies aimed at deepening the school's impact. Yet the state has difficulty discriminating between bureaucratic action that has material effects on headmasters and teachers, versus administrative practices that ritualistically echo the state's signals of modernity and authority.

Prior theories which speak to how and why the state deepens the school's influence assume that political elites have one act, and that this act of rationalizing administration is intentional and effective. I argue that the state's primary point of influence—setting mass conditions—is unintended and difficult to address. Thus it is incomplete to see the teacher as a functional, clearly informed messenger from the state. Yet the teacher, struggling to maintain order and authority under crowded and uncertain conditions, must organize along classic bureaucratic lines. In this way, the teacher serves the fragile state's fundamental objective of signaling mass opportunity within an impersonal organization—such as a classroom replete with secular forms of authority, knowledge, and symbols. Here political elites and local educators arrive at a mutually beneficial agreement, together harmonizing the rules, rituals, and faith which signal how children are to grow up . . . looking more modern.

5

Choice, Community and
The Teaching Craft

> You want to dance across the century,
> Dance across the sea of time . . .
> Dance . . . let your spirit shine!
> —Johnny Clegg and Savuka
> South African musicians

Fact 1. When the first missionaries arrived in Nyasaland, led by
David Livingstone in the mid-nineteenth century, they were perturbed
by how the native villagers built their modest thatched-roof huts. The
damn things were round! And this uncivilized Yao tribe failed to construct their huts in tidy straight rows, scattering them around the village
in seemingly random locations. The Scottish missionaries promptly
demonstrated the magical power (and moral importance) of cornerstones
as they erected their churches. Today, throughout southern Africa,
square houses with sharp corners and sheet-metal roofs hold far more
status than the same "unmodern" huts which made the missionaries so
nervous.[1]

Fact 2. A recent survey found that one-fourth of all Malawian teachers
in some villages still believe in witchcraft. These teachers are privileged
members of the wage-sector, they are relatively well-educated, and they
earnestly present the government's modern curriculum day in and day
out. But when this quarter of the teaching force heads home after work,
they report taking great care not to cross the (always threatening) evil
spirits. And these teachers stay on very good terms with the village
witchdoctor.[2]

These two facts capture the tightening dilemma confronting many fragile Third World states. Political leaders must endorse modernity. The state must attempt to build and reinforce modern bureaucratic institutions. Once Third World nationalists import the Western state, they must try to enforce sharp corners, to impose a rationality which discourages round houses.

Yet the fragile state faces a centrifugal society comprised of disparate communities, holding different languages, family structures, religions, and economic roles. Within such societies, political actors— if they move against round houses too vigorously—risk being seen as particularistic and foreign. Their penetration into plural societies is relentless, sometimes subtle. But the fragile state (by definition) lacks the legitimacy, economic resources, administrative infrastructure, and technical know-how to effectively integrate its fledgling national polity. Political actors simply remain unable to square-off all the rounded edges. Despite relentless attempts at transforming local communities, bewitching persists.

In this final chapter, my first aim is to illuminate the implications of this dilemma for local schools and teachers. This contradiction between the press for modernity versus respect for local pluralism confronts Third World states with particular clarity. Yet central governments throughout Europe and North America also are struggling for legitimacy in the face of growing counterforces: a broadening rainbow of ethnic diversity, an increasing political strength of pluralistic groups, a widening recognition that central bureaucracies erode local community, and a failure of individualistic action (via markets) to address deepening, collectively-held social problems.

State-craft and the Teaching Craft

When the central state's credibility is under fire, political action aimed at linking the school to the local community is very difficult. This is the second major point emphasized in this chapter. The institution of mass schooling is now tightly linked with the state's agenda: building and reinforcing nation-wide loyalties, promising mass opportunity, pushing cultural homogenization, and boosting economic growth and employment within corporate firms and government agencies. Until the school is partially de-coupled from these "national interests," it will remain an object of the central state, not an organization controlled locally, and not one which can serve pluralistic cultural and economic demands. In turn, the teacher will continue to be the objectified instrument of central political actors, not a professional encouraged to improve his or her own craft.

My plea with would-be school reformers is that they understand and respect the Western state's forceful desire to reinforce its own institutional position and authority. The dilemmas and contradictions facing the Western state yield the temperament of a tired child. When provoked the state will strike out, expressing its self-centered will, attempting to control the situation. Past efforts to craft a state (and school) more respectful of local community often have been attempted naively, ignoring the state's resilient capacity to protect and bolster its own strength at the center. Contradictions facing the state *do* present opportunities for moving away from its central preoccupation with cultural homogenization and economic expansion. Yet pressures on the Western state to address—both materially and symbolically—serious economic and social problems will continue. These forces may intensify and even originate from the political Left, which by habit often turns to bureaucratic organizations for, and regulatory means of, addressing society's ills.

Throughout this book I have illustrated how the state's earnest attempts to expand and deepen mass schooling stem from distinct ideologies and strong expectations about what modern political elites must deliver. To look modern, they must organize states that help build a nation-wide economy, implant achieved (not ascribed or caste) forms of merit and mobility, and legitimate bureaucratic organizations. In the pursuit of its central agenda, the state must recast how children grow up—modern socialization must be constructed to fit the modern social organization. Thus the state tries to impress fundamental institutional rules: linking job entry to school credentials, setting standardized national exams in the dominant tribe's language, writing a uniform curriculum and creating official knowledge, and intensifying control of what teachers teach and how they behave moment to moment in the classroom.

Thus the *craft*, or regulated *mechanics*, of teaching stems directly from the Western state's own motivations, methods, and frustrated attempts to penetrate and corral pluralistic communities. *Fragile states* are under enormous pressure to look modern and to enact measures which appear to extend educational opportunity and deepen actual effects on children. The 1980s exemplified how even *established states* in the West recurrently face economic and cultural uncertainties. And, as in the case of the United States or Great Britain over the past decade, we vividly saw how the exercise of *state-craft* involves aggressive action upon the *teaching craft*.

Educators talk much about making schools more relevant and accountable to the preferences and needs of local communities. Rhetoric also is heard about nurturing in teachers a stronger sense of professional craft. But such efforts repeatedly are undercut by the impatient central state—anxious to standardize and boost children's performance, to homogenize socialization and language, and to advance *nation-wide* political and economic goals, be they defined as economic expansion, strengthening moral behavior, or providing more equitable opportunity.

How the state defines and legitimates *choice and community* in society shapes the character and sustainability of school reforms. If "choice" is defined by the state as the expansion of mass opportunity within a uniform labor structure and within large firms or government bureaucracies, then a standardized educational system indeed is rational. On the other hand, where inventive states have emphasized the reinforcement of local community, greater power has been awarded to parents, teachers, and principals in fitting the school to local demands. When creative political actors raise local actors' ownership and efficacy, then the professional authority and craft of teachers also receives a boost. We will look at such examples of placing community on an equal footing with mass choice.

Choice Against Community

According to Western political logic, the provision of greater choice is *inversely* related to the strength of local community. In the Third World, this is strikingly clear, and the source of much political anxiety. In the First World, where we are so accepting of the state's advocacy for mass choice, contemporary erosion of local community often goes unnoticed and unquestioned. As detailed in Chapter 2, the modern state unabashedly works to break down local institutions and affiliations: the church, village governance, and the family. These are all stigmatized as being particularistic and "traditional." Modern forms of achievement and virtue, defined and sanctioned by the state, become embedded within mass schooling, entry to the wage-sector, and status within bureaucratic organizations. The individual gains status in modern society by disavowing local loyalties and pledging allegiance to nation-wide organizations—the school, the state, and the big firm.

Historically, in the Third World, few civic affiliations existed above the tribal level, prior to the coming of the Western state. The opposite historical sequence has occurred in European society. Civic associations pre-date corporate firms and the central state. But their authority often erodes as central political agencies surround, internalize, and cool out plural politics and culture. As Samuel Bowles and Herbert Gintis put it, liberal capitalism (even in the affluent West) has produced "a vast political waste-land between the individual and the state."[3]

In the Third World, the lack of an organized civic territory, located between local village and the bureaucratic central state, leads to a sharp and highly constrained choice for parents and youths. After leaving school youngsters must choose between the particularistic village and the rationalized modern city. There are few economic opportunities or social networks that lie between the two spheres. Rural people and urban slum-dwellers do often participate economically in both worlds. But this is an illegitimate way to live; its status is much lower than the lifestyle of those who have fully entered the wage-sector, the modern world. Few civic institutions exist within which these groups can help themselves. They become objects of the state's welfare strategies; they come to be seen by political elites as "peripheral" or "at risk" groups who need the remedies offered by the central state.

Why is the erosion of local community accepted by most groups and individuals? Mainly because the Western state promises a lot in return. The *individual* citizen who displays loyalty is given a variety of rights. The state also alleges that economic opportunities will open up for those children that go through mass schooling, the modern form of socialization. Diversity among communities is *tolerated* when Third World states are secure enough to approach democratic norms present in the West. But the tolerance of pluralistic differences among local communities is very different from respecting or even serving diversity. The Western tradition is to accept certain differences, then to define uniform individual rights which encourage youths to join nation-wide organizations and to affiliate with a single national culture. The individual buys this lexicon of rights and the promise of broader economic choices by surrendering social links to local community. Mass schooling, of course, plays the key role in re-socializing children away from local loyalties.

In the Third World—i.e., in fragile states—the Western conception of individualistic choice is pushed by two intertwined forces. Once political leaders and their agencies promise political rights and economic opportunity, they must deliver. As the state looks more modern, it cues high expectations that mass opportunity and choice will be broadened. And independent of state action, aspiring capitalists and the middle class vocally demand these social and economic "entitlements" when the state fails to deliver promptly. Of course, many autocratic Third World states have yet to deliver either democratic ideals or steady economic growth. These states tend to be especially brittle, politically dependent upon narrow economic interests or tribal groups. But the long-term legitimacy of such states is threatened if they appear to be more *pre-modern* than modern. The few political leaders with whom I have discussed this issue are conscious of both the limited popular rights and opportunities made available by the state, and the peoples' awareness that their government falls short of being truly modern. But many fragile states can move only so far along the path toward Western ideals, given the narrowness of their political base and the severe economic realities which lag way behind popular expectations.

Ironically where social choices and economic opportunities are highly constrained or eroding, local community is reinforced. We can clearly observe this in a growing number of African countries where school enrollments are erratic or eroding, following the steady decline of the modern wage-sector. Parents observe that fewer jobs are available in the towns and cities.[4] And since the Western state (and its international agencies) usually link mass schooling to *economic* outcomes, parents rationally ask: Why should I keep my children in school if there are no jobs to be found? Why not increase their work around the house, weeding the garden, carrying water, and tending their younger siblings? Again, the inverse relationship between choice and community places the fragile state in a paradoxical vice.

The Modern State's Declining Legitimacy

The dilemma facing established Western states differs somewhat from that which confronts more brittle Third World states. European and North American states have delivered more strongly on individualistic rights. Private markets and state advancement of capitalist economic rules have yielded wide economic choices for certain social groups. Yet the long term legitimacy or perceived relevance of the central state is eroding. The fact that now just one half of all American adults vote in presidential elections—a central act of membership in the formal polity—is commonly cited yet remains quite telling.

Established Western societies are no longer optimistic that the welfare state can effectively assist, or even understand, the problems facing working-class and low-income groups. An increasingly educated middle class grows tired of the rhetoric and regulatory methods of the corporate state. Individualistic market rules and materialist preoccupations, earlier advanced by the classically liberal state, are gaining supporters from a widening range of social classes which see less and less meaning in centralized versions of the modern state. Ironically, unbridled action by individuals and firms intensifies a variety of social and economic ills which then require stronger action by centralized agencies: poverty and intensifying social class divisions, worsening environmental degradation, further erosion of local community and a resulting rise in alienation and personal disconnectedness.[5]

When the Western state is under fire—and corresponding faith in individualistic action and market remedies deepens—mass schooling becomes even more credible. From the state's perspective, secular schooling provides the meritocratic structure within which each individual can prove his or her intellectual acumen, economic productivity, and moral virtue. So embedded in the Western psyche, the school institution appears as *structureless*, neutrally providing educational opportunity, job mobility, and social status. These individualistic pursuits appear to require a minimal role for the centralized state and, of course, allow detachment of the individual from "old-fashioned" forms of community: family, church, neighborhood, ethnic leadership, and even one's own mother tongue.

Countering the traditional Western state are a variety of cultural forces that bring even greater uncertainty to centralized political actors. For example, growing respect for ethnic diversity, disinterest in big bureaucracies and their regulatory methods, rediscovery of local neighborhood, and growing disaffection with a colorless national culture all act to push political elites to rethink the state's credible role. As the interests, motivations, and methods of the central state are increasingly questioned among a majority of the polity, how might state actors construct a more useful role for their political institutions?

Western political agencies have historically gained institutional strength when they have unified disparate tribes into one nation-wide polity *and* simultaneously advanced economic freedom for those individuals and firms that hold sufficient resources to benefit from materialist liberty. Yet the post-modern individual finds that he or she can no longer snuggle-up and be warmed by a homogenous national culture or a fully integrated market. And a resurgent desire for communal ties is rebuffed as long as economic opportunity and social status are embedded in large corporate actors, rather than more human-scale organizations.

Community and the Teaching Craft

In some cases the state's fragility opens opportunities for strengthening community and the teaching craft. First, let's pin down this potential link between community-building and advancing the craft of teaching. As put in the negative above, as long as mass schooling is driven by the central state's agenda, obsessed with nation-building and cultural integration, teaching will be defined as a mechanical process to be shaped by the regulatory and symbolic action of political actors and education bureaucrats. Yet, when the quality of schooling is directly connected with the demands of local communities—their local values, social rules, knowledge, and economy—then teaching will more likely be seen as a craft. What is taught, and the social rules of achievement, must then be determined collaboratively by civic activists and the professional teacher.[6]

To illustrate the link between state action and the school's posture in community-building, let's go back to Chapter 3. There we explored four key contradictions related to *how* the state constructs, then attempts to reinforce, mass schooling. Let's frame these political methods for shaping the *role, tools, and craftfulness of teachers* in terms of their capacity to erode, or reinforce, local community.

—The state eagerly acts *to expand formal schooling* to ethnic groups on the polity's periphery and to new age-groups across all social classes (most recently, "preschool-aged" children). Mass expansion inevitably threatens *educational quality*. In the short-run the state must attend to the political and largely symbolic task of building more schools, looking more inclusive and more modern. But as quality becomes a salient issue, the relevance of particular knowledge and forms of literacy pushed by the central state becomes a major issue for plural communities. On a parallel level, the teacher's professional capacities and agility (or mechanical compliance with the state's official curriculum) become major issues within teacher organizations.

—The state must attend first to the *educational demands of elites and the restless middle class*. Yet economic growth depends on boosting productivity in *rural areas* and on lessening the welfare demands of *disenfranchised urban groups*. As centralized technical solutions fail, political innovators have begun suggesting how the state might nurture greater local ownership of social organizations, including the schools. In much of the Third World, education ministries are struggling to decentralize school management, "ruralize" elements of the curricula, and encourage communities to invest more of their own labor and monetary resources in their local schools.

—As mass schooling expands and the state's fiscal resources weaken, the *working conditions of teachers deteriorate*. The central state's habitual reliance on regulatory and rhetorical remedies for declining educational quality also erodes the craftful facets of teaching. In the Third World teachers rarely have acted as professionals. Poorly prepared teachers continue to be sent into overcrowded classrooms with routinized scripts for how they can hold the attention of fifty to one hundred children. Recent efforts aimed at raising pedagogical quality, however, are encouraging teachers to craft their own, more complex strategies for engaging and motivating children. Boosting the role of the headmaster, and seeing the school as the key organizational unit, not the central ministry of education, are necessary steps toward linking the school to the community.

—The state's *exercise of modern (bureaucratic) management* wins political points. Witness the eagerness of many state-level governments in the United States to "tighten up" on the accountability of local educators, urging higher standards for school graduation, narrowing what and how teachers teach, even standardizing the pedagogical behaviors of new teachers.[7] Yet evidence demonstrating that such regulatory remedies boost teacher effectiveness or student achievement

143

is very difficult to find. Thoughtful political leaders, then, engage in reforms that encourage local ownership and accountability, or urge education ministries to *illustrate* effective practices without imposing them. Links between these strategies and improving either the craft of teaching or the motivation of students are equally unclear. But the movement of authority and participation (maybe even technical know-how) down to the community level is a necessary first step. Here the central state offers *civic incentives*, encouraging parents and community activists to organize around, and debate, the question of how to socialize their own children.[8]

Indeed, such green sprouts of grass continue to push up through the concrete.[9] Windows of opportunity are spotted and pursued by inventive political actors and educators. In the United States, for example, various efforts are being undertaken by a panoply of groups which encourage local schools and teachers to serve the interests of *community*, not only to broaden materialist *choices* in the name of mass opportunity. Several state governments are allocating funds and authority to school-level councils. The functions and decisions over which principals, teachers, and parents can actually exercise control often remain narrow. But the move away from centralized authority is a significant step.[10]

The most recent push for school reform in the West has come in two waves. First, bureaucratic progressives argued that teachers should teach a narrower curriculum, emphasizing "the basics." The individual child should then compete more vigorously to do better on standardized exams, which of course can only assess a narrow range of acquired knowledge. But then, educators and more thoughtful political actors remembered that the development of analytic proficiency, problem-solving competencies, even enjoyment of ideas and literature, involve more complex intellectual skills. And engaging children at deeper levels of cognition and motivation requires more complex ways of organizing classroom instruction, moving beyond routinized pedagogical scripts that are too often reinforced by bureaucratic progressives (as we saw vividly in Chapter 4).[11]

A critical subplot runs under this dialectic between the "back to basics" and the "cognitive complexity" camps: Should teachers encourage individual competition and atomistic ways of learning, or should children be taught cooperative forms of action and work? Indeed the *cooperative learning* field has become a large movement in the United States, a civic organization if you will.[12] This movement has gained credibility as we learn more about how Japanese teachers in the early grades encourage cooperation and reward the work-group's performance, not the individual child.[13]

In addition, some American educators argue that we should respect the multi-dimensional competencies of children. In the classroom, children who are not performing well in the "Three R's" reveal low general ability in the eyes of their fellow students. If different ways of doing well can be structured, the children's own pecking order is scrambled. Every child is then viewed at being good at some tasks and only fair on others. Multi-faceted forms of achievement and expression would reduce the frequency with which minority children are stigmatized, and simply recognize that diverse communities reproduce plural skills and knowledge.[14]

Teachers will not invest in the community which surrounds their school until their own role is seen as important and craftful. Most often, teachers are the *objects* of school reform. Only rarely are teachers encouraged to author and craft their own improvements. The bureaucratic structure of schooling rarely rewards excellent teachers. Too often, teacher unions' concern with equitable treatment has limited innovative career structures and professional advancement. The only way to move ahead is to leave the classroom and enter administration. Only under the logic of Western modernity would institutions assign positive meaning and material rewards to those who leave the children behind.

Nor will teachers and schools work in the service of community until children are seen as resourceful, inventive creatures. The political regulators of mass schooling rarely take seriously the romantic side of Western commitments and ideals regarding individual development. Too often children simply become the objects of schooling, implicitly passive and incompetent beings that must be filled with knowledge and externally molded to fit normative social rules. Even in affluent nations, "development" rarely means giving the child space to craft his or her own learning. Of course, every community interested in reinforcing its local knowledge and cultural rules will structure the socialization process. But variation is very wide in the degree to which the child is regulated or given a spacious achievement structure in which his or her own curiosities and ways of feeling efficacious can be pursued. Our capacity to develop truly democratic community within a pluralistic society is manifest in our sensitivity to each child's strengths and resourcefulness.

Finally, I emphasize that we should not naively view *decentralization* as a universal panacea for all situations. Local control often has narrowed democratic participation and has reinforced inequality. Culturally dominant tribes and social classes can control *local* political and educational processes just as narrowly, perhaps more stridently, as centralized political and economic organizations. Nor should we assume that local actors—be they school boards, teachers, or parents—hold more technical know-how than do central bureaucrats. (Too often, however, we automatically postulate the opposite.) At least under local forms of authority, educational improvements must first gain credibility and ownership from those who must implement the change within schools and classrooms.

It is impossible, within this concluding chapter, to demonstrate that these alternative ways of organizing schools will help reconstruct community and, in turn, renew the craftful character of teaching. Yet (my own) rhetoric aside, these examples do illustrate that some states are strengthening the authority of local actors and organizations. Only within a more coherent and accessible local community can teachers expect to advance their craft.

A Gentle, Illustrative State?

One must ask whether the recurring, often loud discourse over educational reform highlights the school's importance in advancing choice, *not* community. Whether your ear is turned to political debates in the United States, Europe, or southern Africa, the most vocal leaders are claiming that more and better schooling will boost economic growth, international competitiveness, and social mobility. The modern way of growing up, and the state's relentless efforts to expand and deepen mass schooling, are motivated by a desire to expand individual choice and national status. The strengthening of local community, beyond rhetorical reliance on market solutions, is far down the state's list of priorities. The top items on the political agenda—national integration, equity along economic gauges, freedom of corporate actors, and the rationalization of social life—consistently eclipse plural economic and cultural concerns.

Can we realistically expect the Western state to turn seriously to the issue of community? Why would political actors at the center risk undercutting their own nexus of authority and resources by strengthening pluralistic villages and neighborhoods? Can the state become a gentle illustrator—a more craftful sculptor of democratic economic practices, technical innovations, personal forms of local organization, and more motivating ways of teaching our children?

One predictable response is: "Let's just keep the state out of it." Critics of government contend that deeper cultural pressures already are moving institutions in these post-bureaucratic, democratic directions. [15] But such cultural optimism may be naive. Demands on the state to further centralize and intensify bureaucratic remedies recurrently arise during periods of economic uncertainty. Pressure for strong state action also will build as certain social problems worsen, be it the growing gulf between rich and poor or relentless environmental decline.

Like the local school, the modern state increasingly is a contested institutional territory. In many Third World countries, especially in Latin America, we see a well-educated middle class pushing for democratic rights, even occasionally advocating greater local control. But they also demand that central governments allocate welfare entitlements, manage the economy better, and provide more equitable mobility. It may be a long time before the Western state moves seriously away from central transmission of bureaucratic remedies and symbolic admonitions.

We know very little about how to mobilize political agencies to help link the community, the school, and the craft of teaching. What organizational and technical strategies work and under what conditions? In the Third World we *do* know that the contradictions besetting the fragile state can rise up and smash the best of intentions. I have repeatedly seen, for instance, attempts in Africa at improving the quality of rural primary schools swamped by the stronger tide of building more classrooms or schools for urban elites. It is unlikely that centralized fragile states will think about legitimating and rebuilding local community until the political structure becomes more confident and operates on a wider base of institutional support.

Thinking back to Chapter 1, the fragile state is characterized by (a) interdependencies with other organizations and interest groups, (b) little discretion over what it must promise to deliver, especially mass opportunity within a homogenous culture, (c) a weak administrative infrastructure and only slight penetration into a strong, diverse society, and (d) constrained technical knowledge regarding how to spark local economic and social innovations. Brittle states spend full-time struggling to get their own institutional acts together. Efforts to strengthen local community run counter to the construction of legitimacy, the accumulation of resources, and the development of technical know-how *at the center*. Would-be reformers seeking to strengthen local organization must respect the strong forces that circle around and within the Western state. To ignore this structure means that well-intentioned educational reforms will be worn down over time.

On the other hand, if the state's frailties are clearly seen and respected, school reforms may boost the political center's legitimacy *and* enhance the school's catalytic role in strengthening local community. The demise of central regulation and empty political symbols need not threaten the post-modern state. As we have seen, several inventive states—in First and Third Worlds alike—already are shifting authority to the local school and its surrounding community, illustrating effective pedagogical practices, and trying to broaden the craft of teaching.

If such creative strategies work to motivate teachers and to raise children's achievement, political actors can share in receiving well-deserved credit. Teachers will more likely define their work as a complex, inventive craft, not simply a routinized script dictated from above. And children will do more than merely grow up modern. Just maybe their learning and curiosities, rather than being stunted by mechanical classroom rules and official knowledge, will sprout more heartily from a fertile, warmer community over which teachers, parents, and children themselves feel greater control.

Notes

Series Editor's Introduction

1. See Michael W. Apple, "Redefining Equality," *Teacher's College Record*, 90 (Winter, 1988), pp. 167–184.
2. Samuel Bowles and Herbert Gintis, *Schooling in Capitalist America* (New York: Basic Books, 1976).
3. Michael W. Apple, "Standing on the Shoulders of Bowles and Gintis: Class Formation and Capitalist Schools", *History of Education Quarterly*, 28 (Summer 1988), pp. 231–241.
4. I have discussed this in considerably more detail in a series of volumes. See Michael W. Apple, *Ideology and Curriculum*, second edition, (New York: Routledge, 1990), *Education and Power* (New York: Routledge, 1985), and *Teachers and Texts: A Political Economy of Class and Gender Relations in Education* (New York: Routledge, 1988). See also, Michael W. Apple and Lois Weis, eds., *Ideology and Practice in Schooling* (Philadelphia: Temple University Press, 1983).
5. Martin Carnoy, *The State and Political Theory* (Princeton: Princeton University Press, 1984).
6. Roger Dale, *The State and Education Policy* (Bristol, PA: The Open University Press, 1989).
7. For an interesting application of this approach, one that focuses on the development of Western schooling, see John Boli, *New Citizens for a New Society* (New York: Pergamon, 1989).
8. Apple, *Education and Power* and Apple, *Teachers and Texts*.
9. See, e.g., Colin Lankshear with Moira Lawler, *Literacy, Schooling and Revolution* (Philadelphia: Falmer Press, 1987) and Didacus Jules, "Building Democracy: Content and Ideology in Grenadian Educational Textbooks" in Michael W. Apple and Linda K. Christian-Smith, eds., *The Politics of the Textbook* (New York: Routledge, 1991).

1   A Faithful Yet Rocky Romance Between State and School

1. Here I use the term "state" to signify formal agencies of secular government, be they operating within a national capital or local town. "Polity" refers to the political institutions, economic organizations, and civic mores which organize individuals within the Western nation-state. Political elites or leaders, through agencies of the state help define and legitimate the social rules, ideals, and rituals of membership that operate in the broader polity.

2. For historical review, see John Boli, Francisco Ramirez and John W. Meyer, "Explaining the Origins and Expansion of Mass Education," *Comparative Education Review*, Vol. 29 (1985), pp. 145–70. For a historical perspective from Europe, see Bruce Fuller, Jerald Hage, Maurice Garnier and Max Sawicky, "Constructing the French State, Building Village Schools," (Harvard University, draft manuscript, 1990).

3. Under the Reagan Administration United States schools were continually prodded to strengthen both the moral fiber and the economic productivity of youths. See especially, *A Nation at Risk* (Washington, D.C.: U.S. Government Printing Office, 1983). State pressure on schools to address the moral character of children, of course, is not new. For a historical review of the U.S. situation, see David Tyack and Elizabeth Hansot, *Managers of Virtue* (New York: Basic Books, 1982).

4. Enrollment data are obtained from John W. Meyer and Michael Hannan eds., *National Development and the World System: Educational, Economic, and Political Change, 1950–1970* (Chicago: University of Chicago Press, 1979); UNESCO, *Trends in School Enrollment 1950–2000* (Paris: Office of Statistics, 1983).

5. For analyses of the erosion of school quality and how governments react, see Bruce Fuller, "Is Primary School Quality Eroding in the Third World?" *Comparative Education Review*, Vol. 30 (1986), pp. 491–507; Marlaine Lockheed and Adriaan Verspoor, *Improving Primary Education in Developing Countries* (Washington, D.C.: World Bank, 1990).

6. For an international example, see Harold Stevenson's recently celebrated study on school effectiveness, "Classroom Behavior and Achievement of Japanese, Chinese, and American Children," *Advances in Instructional Psychology*, Vol. 3 (1986), pp. 153–191. For a variety of government strategies aimed at boosting "school effectiveness," advanced by state governors in the U.S. with modest infusions of political-economic values, see National Governors' Association, *Results in Education 1989* (Washington, D.C., 1989).

7. "Bureaucratic rules," defined here in Weberian terms, include hierarchical levels of authority, universal and specific criteria for judging the individual's technical skills and social status, impersonal social relations based on one's organizational role, and routinization of work into predictable tasks, based

on universal "facts" and sacred forms of knowledge. Such rationalization is manifest both in the technical structure and the deeper "moral order," in that forms of authority, rules, and cultural commitments reinforcing this structure become sacred and unquestioned.

8. For a historical review from the U.S., see David Tyack, *One Best System* (Cambridge, Mass.: Harvard University Press, 1974). My Chapter 3 in the present book looks in depth at how one east African state exerts administrative pressure on local schools and teachers.

9. In addition to Tyack, *One Best System*, see Chapter 4 of the present volume for one case from the Third World.

10. Robert Everhart, *Reading, Writing, and Resistance: Adolescence and Labor in a Junior High School* (Boston: Routledge and Kegan Paul, 1983). The institutionalization of once novel "social facts" is described in Emile Durkheim, *Education and Sociology*, trans. by Sherwood Fox (Glencoe, Illinois: The Free Press, 1956).

11. Case studies from the Third World are carefully reported in Joel Migdal, *Strong Societies and Weak States* (Princeton, N.J.: Princeton University Press, 1987).

12. Earlier literature on the Western state is reviewed in Theda Skocpol and Edwin Amenta, "States and Social Policies," *Annual Review of Sociology*, Vol. 12 (1986), pp. 131–57; Martin Carnoy, *The State and Political Theory*. More textured understandings of the state's complexities, both its internal processes and its interdependencies with other organizations, are emerging. Most notably, see Claus Offe, *Contradictions of the Welfare State*, trans. by John Keane (Cambridge, Mass.: MIT Press, 1984). More complex views of the state's influence on schools appear in Michael Apple and Lois Weis, "Ideology and Practice in Schooling: A Political and Conceptual Introduction," in Apple and Weis eds., *Ideology and Practice in Schooling* (Philadelphia: Temple University Press, 1983).

13. A variety of theorists have assumed that the same forces and processes operate on the expansion and the deepening of mass schooling, including Samuel Bowles and Herbert Gintis, *Schooling in Capitalist America: Educational Reform and the Contradictions of Economic Life* (New York: Basic Books, 1976). For a more recent review of theoretical developments in this area, see Harvey Kantor and Robert Lowe, "Empty Promises: An Essay Review," *Harvard Educational Review*, Vol. 57 (1987), pp. 68–76.

14. See Offe, *Contradictions of the Welfare State* ; Offe, "Structural Problems of the Capitalist State," in Klaus von Beyme, ed., *German Political Studies*, Vol. 1 (London: Sage Publications, 1974), pp. 31–58.

15. For review, see Carnoy, *The State and Political Theory*. Also, see Max Weber, G. Roth and W. Schluchter, eds., *Max Weber's Vision of History* (Berkeley: University of California Press, 1979).

16. The central state's accommodation to local authority and school commitments was a major issue in Europe during the nineteenth century. In France,

for instance, see Roger Thabault, *Education and Change in a Village Community*: *Mazieres-en-Gatine, 1848–1914*, trans. by Peter Tregear (London: Routledge and Kegan Paul, 1971). For Third World cases, see Migdal, *Strong Societies and Weak States*. An engaging, emic view of one Zimbabwean family is reported in Tsitsi Dangarembga, *Nervous Conditions* (Seattle: Seal Press, 1988).

17. Contrasting views of the state are reviewed quite well in Carnoy, *The State and Political Theory*. For conflicting views of the state's role in Western society, see Robert Nisbet, *A History of the Idea of Progress* (New York: Basic Books, 1980).

18. John W. Meyer, "The Effects of Education as an Institution," *American Journal of Sociology*, Vol. 83 (1977), pp. 55–77; John W. Meyer and Michael Hannan, eds., *National Development and the World System*: *Educational, Economic, and Political Change, 1950–1970* (Chicago: University of Chicago Press, 1979); George Thomas and John W. Meyer, "The Expansion of the State," in Ralph Turner and James Short, Jr., eds. *Annual Review of Sociology*, Vol. 10 (1984), pp. 461–82; Boli etal., "Explaining the Origins and Expansion of Mass Education."

19. For the case of the U.S. in the nineteenth century, see John W. Meyer, David Tyack, Joane Nagel, and Audri Gordon, "Public Education as Nation-Building in America," *American Journal of Sociology*, Vol. 85 (1979), pp. 591–613. For France, see Fuller et al., "Constructing the French State, Building Village schools."

20. For review, see Lockheed and Verspoor, *Improving Primary Education in Developing Countries*.

21. See James S. Coleman, "Social Capital in the Creation of Human Capital," *American Journal of Sociology*, Vol. 94 (1988), pp. S95–S120.

22. See Durkheim, *Education and Sociology*, trans. by Sherwood Fox (Glencoe, Illinois: Free Press, 1956); Robert Nisbet, *The Sociology of Emile Durkheim* (New York: Oxford University Press, 1974); Louis Althusser, *"Lenin and Philosophy" and Other Essays* (New York: Monthly Review Press, 1971); Nicos Poulantzas, *Political Power and Social Classes* (London: New Left Books, 1974).

23. See Michael Pusey, *Key Sociologists*: *Jurgen Habermas* (London: Tavistock Publications, 1987).

24. See Migdal, *Strong Societies and Weak States*.

25. For reviews of implicit contradictions in Western political and social philosophy, see J. Bowen and P. Hobson, *Theories of Education: Studies in Western Educational Thought* (New York: Wiley and Sons, 1974); Nisbet, *A History of the Idea of Progress*.

26. See Thomas and Meyer, "The Expansion of the State."

27. I agree with active-state theorists that, under some conditions, political elites can move independently to build or reinforce other institutions. See Peter Evans, Dietrich Rueschemeyer, and Theda Skocpol, *Bringing the*

State Back In (New York: Cambridge University Press, 1985). For the historical case of France, see Maurice Garnier, Jerald Hage, and Bruce Fuller, "The Strong State, Social Class, and Controlled School Expansion in France, 1881–1975," *American Journal of Sociology*, Vol. 95 (September 1989), pp. 279–306. For a Third World case, see Bruce Fuller, Maurice Garnier, and Jerald Hage, "State Action and Labor Structure Change in Mexico," *Social Forces*, Vol. 68 (1990) pp. 1165–89.

28. The state can use the school as a conservative *or* as a progressive force. Most European and North American writers emphasize how the school reinforces dominant economic and moral commitments. But in these settings society is largely rationalized and accepting of Western political-economic ideals. In Third World settings, the state employs the school to move tribal networks toward Western commitments and forms of organization. Fragile states frequently are caught in the contradiction of wanting to bring modern economic progress without becoming excessively Western in terms of social values. This awkward pursuit of state and educational policy is seen in young socialist polities and within states which attempt to retain traditional moral or religious commitments.

2   What Drives the Expansion and Deepening of Mass Schooling?

1. Early Greek literature talks of how formal agencies of the state (or government) seek to pull in the individual as a citizen or member of the modern polity. But the distinction between actors in government organizations versus membership in the broader polity is important. In addition, *civic* life within the polity is distinct from *private* life at home, according to Western conceptions. For review, see J. Bowen and P. Hobson, *Theories of Education: Studies in Western Educational Thought* (New York: Wiley and Sons, 1974). For Marx, in contrast, "civil society" or the polity was comprised of the basic structure of production and trade—that is, rationalized social relations now centered on economic expansion. For review, see Norberto Bobbio, "Gramsci and the Conception of Civil Society," in Chantal Mouffe, ed., *Gramsci and Marxist Theory* (London: Routledge and Kegan Paul, 1979).

2. North American educators' early twentieth-century mimicry of factory organization and their ideological preoccupation with the "efficiency" of public schools is detailed in David Tyack, *One Best System* (Cambridge, Mass.: Harvard University Press, 1974)

3. Within the functionalist framework, modern practices and ideology connote (a) beliefs, skills, or rationalized technology that aid the individual's contribution to economic production (within a free market or bureaucratic firm),

or (b) social action linked to faith in the individual's potential and autonomy, thereby signalling membership in the modern tribe (or polity).

4. Functionalist views of socializing the child to fit the modern political-economy are provided in Emile Durkheim, *Education and Sociology*, trans. by Sherwood Fox (Glencoe, Illinois: The Free Press, 1956); Talcott Parsons, *The Structure of Social Action* (Glencoe, Illinois: The Free Press, 1949); Pierre Bourdieu and Jean-Claude Passeron *Reproduction in Education, Society and Culture*, trans. by Richard Nice (London: Sage, 1977). For a review of how early modern states sought to individualize property rights and labor contracts, see York Bradshaw, "Urbanization and Underdevelopment: A Global Study of Modernization, Urban Bias, and Economic Dependency," *American Sociological Review*, Vol. 52 (1988), pp. 224–239.

5. When I say, "sacred symbols," I draw from Durkheim's point that certain actions or artifacts take on unquestioned meaning and value. Among elites in east Africa, for instance, competence in speaking English, having a TV, or now a VCR, are important rituals that *signal* status and membership in the modern polity, independent of their actual economic importance.

6. Parallels between the God-individual connection and the State-individual link are discussed in, Lewis Spitz, *The Protestant Reformation, 1517–1559* (New York: Harper and Row, 1985). Also see George Thomas and John W. Meyer, "The Expansion of the State," in Ralph Turner and James Short, Jr., eds., *Annual Review of Sociology*, Vol. 10 (1984), pp. 461–82.

7. Plato's writings talked (in negative tones) about the limitations of kinship bonds. Instead he advocated modern forms of social and political organization. Much later, Hegel argued that the civic polity was the preeminent collectivity: "The Nation State in its substantive rationality. . is therefore the absolute power on earth. . wherein individuals find their essential nature expressed." Hegel's position is reviewed in Robert Nisbet, *A History of the Idea of Progress* (New York: Basic Books, 1980), pp. 277, 281. Also see John Boli, Francisco Ramirez and John W. Meyer, "Explaining the Origins and Expansion of Mass Education," *Comparative Education Review*, Vol. 29 (1985), pp. 145–70.

8. See Durkheim, *Education and Sociology*. For an early European case (from France), see Barnett Singer, *Village Notables in 19th Century France: Priests, Mayors, Schoolmasters* (Albany, New York: State University of New York Press, 1983).

9. See Samuel Bowles and Herbert Gintis, *Schooling in Capitalist America: Educational Reform and the Contradictions of Economic Life* (New York: Basic Books, 1976). A careful review of neo-marxist theory appears in Martin Carnoy, *The State and Political Theory* (Princeton, N.J.: Princeton University Press, 1984).

10. See Nisbet, *A History of the Idea of Progress*.

11. Adam Smith quoted in Carnoy, *the State and Political Theory*, p. 26. and Chapter 1 overview.

12. I will return to the problem of representing the state as a hegemonic, undifferentiated organization. Instead we might see the state as a plural set of actors, each competing for resources and ideological visibility. For instance, we can see officials in education ministries drawing out symbols from the school institution to further their own legitimacy within the state (competing for visibility and resources with other political elites). For now, I stick to the undifferentiated view of the state generally adopted by theorists from all three theoretical camps.

13. See Hal Draper, *Karl Marx's Theory of Revolution, Volume 1: State and Bureaucracy* (New York: Monthly Review Press, 1977).

14. The school may successfully raise the *average* level of literacy or achievement over time. But unless the relative disadvantage of lower class children lessens, elites will disproportionately benefit from school expansion sponsored by the state.

15. See Christopher Jencks etal., *Who Gets Ahead? The Determinants of Economic Success in America* (New York: Basic Books, 1979).

16. See Bruce Fuller, "What School Factors Raise Achievement in the Third World?" *Review of Educational Research*, Vol. 57 (1987), pp. 255–92.

17. Bowles and Gintis, *Schooling in Capital America*. Also see Nicos Poulantzas, *Political Power and Social Classes* (London: New Left Books, 1974). For a more recent and critical review see Harvey Kantor and Robert Lowe, "Empty Promises: An Essay Review," *Harvard Educational Review*, Vol. 57 (1987), pp. 68–76.

18. Robert Dreeben, *On What Is Learned at School* (Addison Wesley, 1968). This emphasis on individualistic achievement may not occur in overcrowded Third World classrooms. Here pupils may simply be processed as a large batch, with little recognition of individual differences (Bowles and Gintis). These conflicting representations suggest very different social rules allegedly found in the classroom. I return to this issue in Chapter Four when we enter African classrooms.

19. Gramsci quoted in Carnoy, *The State and Political Theory*, p. 68. Also see Antonio Gramsci, *Selections from Prison Notebooks* (New York: International Publishers, 1971).

20. Robert Everhart, *Reading, Writing, and Resistance: Adolescence and Labor in a Junior High School* (Boston: Routledge and Kegan Paul, 1983).

21. See Louis Althusser, *Lenin and Philosophy and Other Essays* (New York: Monthly Review Press, 1971); Henry Giroux, *Ideology, Culture, and the Process of Schooling* (Philadelphia: Temple University Press, 1981).

22. The term "institutionalization" is linked to Durkheim's notion that certain behaviors or beliefs, once thought strange or novel, come to be fully accepted. For instance, bringing up children in a factory-like organization called "the government school" was and, in many settings, continues to be seen as a foreign ideal. Over time the desirability of mass schooling becomes institutionalized, an accepted "social fact."

23. See John W. Meyer, "Implications of an Institutional View of Education for the Study of Educational Effects," in Maureen Hallinan, *The Social Organization of Schools* (New York: Plenum Press, 1987). For descriptions of the institutionalization process and the notion of "social facts," see Parsons, *The Structure of Social Action* ; Steven Lukes, *Emile Durkheim: His Life and Work* (London: Allen Lane The Penguin Press, 1973); Lynne Zucker, ed., *Institutional Patterns and Organizations* (New York: Ballinger Publishing, 1988).

24. See Chapters 3 and 4 for an account of how African education ministries and local school inspectors place great importance on these symbols of school quality.

25. For detailed reviews of the world-institution viewpoint see, John W. Meyer and Michael Hannan, eds., *National Development and the World System: Educational, Economic, and Political Change, 1950–1970* (Chicago: University of Chicago Press, 1979); Boli et al., "Explaining the Origins and Expansion of Mass Schooling." Ramirez and Boli discuss the relative strength of ideological action by the central state, versus economic resources and position in the world economy, in pushing school expansion. They examine how political elites in post-Reformation Europe saw the school institution as a symbolically-charged political good as they sought to compete in the European network of states. A nation-state's desire to catch up with stronger states (militarily and culturally) was more strongly related to school expansion than economic resources per se. See Ramirez and Boli, "The Political Construction of Mass Schooling: European Origins and Worldwide Institutionalization," *Sociology of Education*, Vol. 60 (1987), pp. 2–17.

26. John W. Meyer and Brian Rowan, "Institutionalized Organizations: Formal Structure as Myth and Ceremony," *American Journal of Sociology*, Vol. (1977), pp. 340–363. On the intellectual roots of this symbolic view, see Lukes, *Emile Durkheim: His Life and Work.*

27. This official history is detailed in, Kelvin Banda, *A Brief History of Education in Malawi* (Blantyre, Malawi: Dzuka Publishing, 1982).

28. The Ethiopian government's definition of their intriguing curriculum is outlined in, *Marxist-Leninist Ideology in Education: A Contribution to Theory of Socialist Education* (Addis Ababa: Ministry of Education, 1986).

29. See Ramirez and Boli, "The Political Construction of Mass Schooling."

30. See Brian Rowan, "Shamanistic Rituals in Effective Schools," *Issues in Education*, Vol. 2 (1984), pp. 76–87.

31. See Thomas and Meyer, "The Expansion of the State."

32. Boli et al., "Explaining the Origins and Expansion of Mass Schooling." 1985.

33. Margaret Archer, *Social Origins of Educational Systems* (Beverly Hills: Sage Publications, 1979); John Craig, "The Expansion of Education," in David Berliner, *Review of Educational Research* Vol. 9 (Washington, D.C.: American Educational Research Association, 1981), pp. 151–213; Pamela

Walters and Philip O'Connell, "The Family Economy, Work, and Educational Participation in the United States," *American Journal of Sociology*, Vol. 93 (1988), pp. 1116–52.

34. See Gary Becker, *Human Capital* (New York: National Bureau of Economic Research, 1975). For a critical review, see Richard Rubinson, "Class Formation, Politics, and Institutions: Schooling in the United States," *American Journal of Sociology*, Vol. 92 (1986), pp. 519–48.

35. See Meyer and Hannan, eds., *National Development and the World System*.

36. For recent review, see Bruce Fuller, Maurice Garnier and Jerald Hage, "State Action and Labor Structure Change in Mexico," *Social Forces*, Vol. 68 (1990), pp. 1165–89.

37. Richard Rubinson and John Ralph, "Technical Change and the Expansion of Schooling in the United States," *Sociology of Education*, Vol. 57 (1984), pp. 134–52.

38. For a reflective review, see Martin Carnoy and Henry Levin, *Schooling and Work in the Democratic State* (Stanford: Stanford University Press, 1985).

39 See David J. Hogan, *Class and Reform: School and Society in Chicago, 1880–1930* (Philadelphia: University of Pennsylvania Press, 1985; Michael Apple and Lois Weis, eds., *Ideology and Practice in Schooling* (Philadelphia: Temple University Press, 1983).

40. Many families do resist schooling that is controlled by certain elites, be they Muslims opposing secular schooling or Protestants believing that Catholic schools are somehow foreign. In addition, many Third World parents do actively resist schooling after their children reach a certain age, particularly once girls pass puberty. But neither case contradicts the claim that acceptance of formal schooling, of some type and for some age groups, is widespread and deep.

41. Class-based inclusion, rather than exclusion or imposition, is introduced in Ira Katznelson and Aristide Zolberg, eds., *Working-class Formation: 19th Century Patterns in Western Europe and the United States* (Princeton: Princeton University Press, 1986.

42. See Fuller et al., "State Action and Labor Structure Change in Mexico."

43. See Maurice Garnier, Jerald Hage, and Bruce Fuller, "The Strong State, Social Class, and Controlled School Expansion in France, 1881–1975," *American Journal of Sociology*, Vol. 95 (September 1989), pp 279–306.

44. See Rubinson, "Class Formation, Politics, and Institutions: Schooling in the United States."

45. Bruce Fuller and Richard Rubinson, eds., *Conflicting Institutional Forces: The State, School Expansion and Economic Change* (New York: Praeger, in press).

46. See Bruce Fuller et al., "Constructing the French State, Building Village Schools."

47. Economic returns stemming from increases in school quality are reviewed in Bruce Fuller and Stephen Heyneman, "Third World School Quality:

Current Collapse, Future Potential," *Educational Researcher*, Vol. 18 (March 1989), pp. 12–19. Also see Jerald Hage, Maurice Garnier, and Bruce Fuller, "The Active State, Investment in Human Capital, and Economic Growth in France," *American Sociological Review*, Vol. 53 (1988), pp. 824–837.

48. This provocative contrast appears when comparing Martin Carnoy's review of the French structuralists, *The State and Political Theory*, with John W. Meyer's recent paper, "Society without Culture: A 19th Century Legacy," in Francisco Ramirez, ed., *Rethinking the 19th Century: Contradictions and Movements* (New York: Greenwood Press, 1988).

49. Meyer and Hannan, eds., *National Development and the World System*.

50. John W. Meyer, Francisco Ramirez, and Yasemin Soysal, "World Expansion of Mass Education, 1870–1980," paper presented at the American Educational Research Association, San Francisco, 1989.

51. On the conceptual differences among (and measurement issues involved with) school enrollment, attendance, and quality, see Walters and O'Connell, "The Family Economy, Work, and Educational Participation in the United States"; Bruce Fuller, "Is Primary School Quality Eroding in the Third World?" *Comparative Education Review*, Vol. 30 (1986), pp. 491–507.

52. See Boli et al., "Explaining the Origins and Expansion of Mass Schooling."

3 Winding Up Schools: The State Constructs Teachers' Roles and Tools

1. This example is reported by Marlaine Lockheed.

2. Philip Cusick distinguished between the "maintenance" and "production" systems within schools almost 20 years ago, in *Inside High School* (New York: Holt, Rinehart and Winston, 1972). Organizational maintenance is extremely important during early periods of institution-building, absorbing considerable resources from the state. In several Third World countries, enrollments are declining where the school's basic facilities are crumbling, where teachers rarely get paid on time and eventually disappear.

3. James S. Coleman, "Social Capital in the Creation of Human Capital," *American Journal of Sociology*, Vol. 94 (1988), pp. S95–S120.

4. David J. Hogan helped open up the view that schools represent contested territory, fought over by competing ideologies and social classes. See *Class and Reform: School and Society in Chicago, 1880–1930* (Philadelphia: University of Pennsylvania Press, 1985).

5. See Linda M. McNeil, *Contradictions of Control: School Structure and School Knowledge* (New York: Routledge, 1988)

6. See John W. Meyer and Brian Rowan, "The Structure of Educational

Organizations," in Marshall W. Meyer, ed., *Environments and Organizations* (San Francisco: Jossey-Bass, 1978).

7. See Bruce Fuller and Jo Ann Izu, "Explaining School Cohesion: What Shapes the Organizational Beliefs of Teachers?" *American Journal of Education*, Vol. 94 (August 1986), pp. 501–35.

8. Pierre Bourdieu and Jean-Claude Passeron, *Reproduction in Education, Society and Culture*, trans. by Richard Nice (London: Sage, 1977).

9. See the end of Chapter 3 for a summary of one ambitious program in Malawi.

10. My thinking on "selective coupling" across organizational levels is discussed more fully in Bruce Fuller and Sanford M. Dornbusch, "Organizational Construction of Intrinsic Motivation," *Sociological Forum*, Vol. 3 (1988), pp. 1–24.

11. The World Bank's shifting focus is briefly reviewed in Nwanganga Shields, *Malawi: Education Sector Credit, Staff Appraisal Report* (Washington, D.C.: World Bank, 1987). Historical statistics come from Kelvin N. Banda, *A Brief History of Education in Malawi* (Blantyre, Malawi: Dzuka Publishing, 1982). See also, Ministry of Education and Culture, *Malawi: Education Statistics, 1987* (Lilongwe: Government of Malawi, 1987); Stephen Heyneman, "The School as a Traditional Institution in an Underdeveloped Society, *Pedagogica Historica*," Vol. 12 (1972), pp. 460–72.

12. National Statistical Office, *Employment and Earnings Report, 1984–86* (Zomba: Government Printer, 1988).

13. National Statistical Office, *Malawi Family Formation Survey, 1984* (Zomba: Government Printer, 1987).

14. National Statistical Office, *Malawi Population and Housing Census, 1987* (Zomba: Government Printer, 1987). World Bank, *World Development Report, 1989* (Washington, D.C.: World Bank, 1989).

15. Frederic Pryor, *Income Distribution and Economic Development in Malawi: Historical Statistics*, Discussion Paper 36 (Washington D.C.: World Bank, 1988). Also see Jandhyala Tilak, *Financing and Cost Recovery in Social Sectors in Malawi* (Washington, D.C.: World Bank, Southern Africa Department, 1989).

16. For review of contemporary economic and government spending trends, see Bruce Fuller, "Eroding Economy and Declining School Quality: Case of Malawi," *Institute of Development Studies Bulletin*, Vol. 20 (January 1989), pp. 11–16.

17. See Ministry of Education and Culture, *Education Statistics*, 1987; Fuller, "Eroding Economy."

18. These points stem from the work of Jurgen Habermas and Niklas Luhmann, reviewed provocatively in Agnes Heller and Ferene Feher, *The Postmodern Political Condition* (New York: Columbia University Press, 1988).

19. Ministry of Education and Culture, *Education Statistics*, 1987.

20. Bruce Fuller, "What Factors Shape Teacher Quality: Initial Evidence from

Africa," paper presented at the American Educational Research Association, San Francisco, 1989.

21. Ministry of Education and Culture, *Educational Statistics*. For a review of gender inequalities throughout the educational structure, Cameron Bonner and Bruce Fuller, "Malawi Educational Sector Review: Issues and Options for USAID," (Lilongwe: U.S. Agency for International Development, 1989).

22. Ministry of Education and Culture, *Old and New: English in Malawi*, Books 5 and 7 (Blantyre: Dzuka Publishing, 1968).

23. Lev Vygotsky, *Thought and Language*, trans. by Alex Kozulin (Cambridge, Mass.: MIT Press, 1986).

24. Bruce Fuller and Anjimile Kapakasa, "What Factors Shape Teacher Quality? Case of Malawi," *International Journal of Educational Development*, Vol. 10 (1990).

25. Ministry of Education and Culture, *Primary School Quality in Malawi* (Lilongwe: Government of Malawi, 1989).

26. For review, see Marlaine Lockheed and Adriaan Verspoor, *Improving Primary Education in Developing Countries* (Washington, D.C.: World Bank, 1990).

27. National Statistical Office, *Employment and Earnings Report*, 1988.

28. The content of school inspection forms varies across district education offices. The inspection items paraphrased here are included in forms used by inspectors in Lilongwe and Blantyre districts.

29. See Malawi Institute of Education, *Introduction to the Theory and Practice of Teaching* (Blantyre, Malawi: Dzuka Publishing, 1986).

30. For a description of the Canadian-funded headmaster training program, see Pandelis Halamandaris, "Advanced Training of Tutors at Malawi Institute of Education" (Canada: Brandon University, 1989).

31. A brief review of school inspection reports was conducted by the author at Lilongwe urban and rural district offices, 1989.

4 Strong States, Strong Teachers?

1. As in Chapter 1, I use "bureaucratic" to characterize organizations that follow a Weberian form of rationalized rules that govern work and social interaction. This includes authority linked to technical expertise, power arranged hierarchically, tasks and labor subdivided into standardized routines, and evaluation of each individual along universal, narrow, and countable forms of behavior.

2. This aspect of Durkheim's work is discussed in Randall Collins, *Three Sociological Traditions* (Oxford: Oxford University Press, 1985); *Emile Durkheim, Education and Sociology*, trans. by Sherwood Fox (Glencoe, Illinois: The Free Press, 1956).

3. See Bronwyn Davies, *Life in the Classroom and Playground: The Accounts of Primary School Children* (London: Routledge and Kegan Paul, 1982). Robert Everhart, *Reading, Writing, and Resistance: Adolescence and Labor in a Junior High School* (Boston: Routledge and Kegan Paul, 1983). Michael Apple, *Teachers and Texts: A Political Economy of Class and Gender Relations in Education* (New York: Routledge and Kegan Paul, 1986). Henry Giroux, *Ideology, Culture, and the Process of Schooling* (Philadelphia: Temple University Press, 1981). Martin Carnoy and Henry Levin, *Schooling and Work in the Democratic State* (Stanford: Stanford University Press, 1985).

4. See: Michael Apple, *Ideology and Curriculum* (Boston: Routledge, 1979). Martin Carnoy and Henry Levin, *Schooling and Work*. Henry Giroux, *Ideology, Culture*.

5. John W. Meyer and Brian Rowan, "Institutionalized Organizations: Formal Structure as Myth and Ceremony," *American Journal of Sociology*, Vol. 83 (1977), pp. 340–363.

6. Hegel argued that (ideally) the modern state would allow objective freedom through corporate political institutions and encourage particularistic, subjective freedom by the individual within his or her local setting. Through reason and rationalized organizations, the state would ensure tolerance of local diversity and enable the individual (though not necessarily local collectives) to act freely. But when faced with strong balkanization, the central state, for its own survival, may mobilize its institutions to strengthen national integration and leave aside Hegel's idealized respect for local variety. For a thorough review, see John Rundell, *Origins of Modernity: The Origins of Modern Social Theory From Kant to Hegel to Marx* (Madison: University of Wisconsin Press, 1987).

7. Jane Stallings and D. Kaskowitz, *Follow-Through Classroom Observation Evaluation, 1972–1973* (Menlo Park: Stanford Research Institute, 1974). Jane Stallings and others, *A Study of Basic Reading Skills Taught in Secondary Schools* (Menlo Park, Calif.: SRI International, 1978) Carolyn Denham and A. Lieberman, *Time to Learn* (Washington, D.C.: National Institute of Education, 1980). For a concise review, see Nancy Karweit, "Should We Lengthen the School Term?" *Educational Researcher* (June 1985), pp. 9–15. The quote is from the state of Virginia's description of its classroom observation procedure which regulates who can enter teaching. See Division of Professional Development, "Beginning Teacher Assistance Program: What are the Competencies that Teachers will be Expected to Demonstrate?" (Richmond, Virginia: Department of Education, 1986).

8. Harold Stevenson et al., "Classroom Behavior and Achievement of Japanese, Chinese, and American Children," *Advances in Instructional Psychology*, Vol. 3, p. 153–191.

9. For review, see Bruce Fuller, Susan Holloway, Hiroshi Azuma, and Kathleen Gorman, "Contrasting Achievement Rules: Socialization of Japanese

Children at Home and in School," *Research in Sociology of Education and Socialization*, Vol. 6 (Greenwich, Conn.: JAI Press, 1986), pp. 165–201. Catherine Lewis describes how Japanese teachers delegate authority to children's own work groups in "Cooperation and Control in Japanese Nursery Schools," *Comparative Education Review*, Vol. 28 (1984) pp. 69–84.

10. These findings come from the second round of cross-national research by the International Association for the Evaluation of Educational Achievement (IEA), Lorin W. Anderson, Doris W. Ryan, and Bernard J. Shapiro, *The Classroom Environment Study: Teaching for Learning* (Columbia, S.C.: University of South Carolina, 1987).

11. Jean V. Carew and Sara Lawrence Lightfoot, *Beyond Bias: Perspectives on Classrooms* (Cambridge, Mass.: Harvard University Press, 1979). Jeannie Oakes, "Classroom Social Relationships: Exploring the Bowles and Gintis Hypothesis," *Sociology of Education*, Vol. 55 (1982), pp. 197–212.

12. See Paul Willis, *Learning to Labour* (Westmead: Saxon House, 1977). Young children's subtle forms of resistance to classroom organization, including their tireless pursuit of fun, is colorfully described by them in Davies, *Life in the Classroom and Playground*.

13. The most complete papers by Robert Prophet and Patricia Rowell appear in a forthcoming book edited by Conrad Snyder, Jr. and Philemon Ramatsui, *Curriculum in the Classroom* (London: Macmillan Publishers, 1990).

14. Bruce Fuller and Conrad Snyder, Jr., "Vocal Teachers, Silent Pupils? Life in Botswana Classrooms," *Comparative Education Review* (in press).

15. Claus Offe, "Advanced Capitalism and the Welfare State," *Politics and Society* (Summer 1972), pp. 479–88. Claus Offe, *Contradictions of the Welfare State*, trans. by John Keane (Cambridge, Mass.: MIT Press, 1984).

16. More detailed statistical results appear in Bruce Fuller & Anjimile Kapakasa, "What Factors Shape Teacher Quality: Evidence from Malawi," *International Journal of Educational Development*. Marlaine Lockheed, Bruce Fuller, and Ronald Nyirongo, "Family Background and Student Achievement in Thailand and Malawi," *Sociology of Education*, Vol. 62 (1989) pp. 1–17; Ministry of Education & Culture, *Primary School Quality in Malawi* (Lilongwe: Government of Malawi, 1989).

17. In defining "administrative ritual," I again draw on Durkheim's work. Illustrated in this section, political elites and local headmasters engage in many actions that may have little influence in boosting the performance of teachers or pupils. But *as rituals* they signify modern practices and invite school actors to express their loyalty to the state's constructed definition of normative behavior. Administrative rituals, therefore, serve to enhance solidarity and "tribal customs" which bridges the central state (or education ministry) and local school staff.

18. In another teacher's classroom, I observed a civics lecture on how the lack of "ethnic cooperation" between tribes hampered "national unity."

Interestingly, the teacher's lecture was given completely in English, despite the fact that the children's comprehension of Chichewa was visibly better.

19. Anderson et al., *The Classroom Environment Study.*
20. Davies, *Life in the Classroom and Playground.*
21. See note 2 above for the present chapter. Also see Talcott Parsons, *The Structure of Social Action* (Glencoe, Illinois: The Free Press, 1949).
22. Philip Cusick, *Inside High School* (New York: Holt, Rinehart and Winston, 1972).
23. Let's frame this case of language policy within Durkheim's earlier work in nineteenth-century Europe. Concerned over the balkanized character of the French republic, Durkheim spoke of the need to construct "collective representations," that is, the institutionalization of shared ideologies and symbols. Latter-day functionalists tend to ignore *how* the modern state attempts to institutionalize Western ideals and rules, especially within the Third World and plural societies where the central state's pitch is often seen as ideological and illegitimate. European structuralists, though working from a critical perspective, assume high levels of institutionalization. While often true within industrialized countries, declining legitimacy of governments in the West and the ongoing fragility of Third World states demonstrate that "deep structures" are neither deep nor static. Ann Swidler's work is especially relevant here. She examines how (institutionalized) cultural "traditions" can stem from, or turn into, obtrusive "ideology" during periods of rapid change. See Swidler, "Culture in Action: Symbols and Strategies," *American Sociological Review*, Vol. 51 (1986), pp. 273–286.
24. *Old and New: English in Malawi, Book 7* (Blantyre, Malawi: Dzuka Publishing, 1982).
25. Basil Bernstein, *Class, Codes and Control: Towards a Theory of Educational Transmissions, Vol. 3* (London: Routledge and Kegan Paul, 1975).
26. See Everhart, *Reading, Writing, and Resistance.*

5 Choice, Community and the Teaching Craft

1. Landeg White, *Magomero: Portrait of an African Village* (Cambridge, U.K.: Cambridge University Press, 1987).
2. J. D. Makombe, "Role Concepts of Christian and Non-Christian Primary School Teachers," unpublished masters thesis, University of Malawi, Chancellor College, 1982.
3. Samuel Bowles and Herbert Gintis, *Democracy and Capitalism: Property, Community, and Contradictions of Modern Social Thought* (New York: Basic Books, 1987).
4. Studies conducted with governments by the U.S. Agency for International

Development, UNESCO, and the World Bank have documented that primary or secondary enrollments (in absolute numbers or as a proportion of the age cohort) declined in Mali, Somalia, Nigeria, Malawi and Kenya over the 1980s.

5. The modern state's eroding legitimacy (in west European settings) is discussed in Claus Offe, *Contradictions of the Welfare State*, trans. by John Keane (Cambridge, Mass.: MIT Press, 1984.)

6. The school organization can serve the community-building process in ways that are unrelated to the teaching craft. For instance, school-level councils may focus on many organizational maintenance issues, from improving facilities to fund raising. Yet these decision-making structures and the authority entrusted in local actors is a necessary (albeit insufficient) step toward linking the teaching craft to local social and economic demands.

7. A number of state-level departments of education in the United States now prescribe the "competencies" or standardized behaviors that all new teachers must demonstrate in the classroom before being licensed. For the fascinating case of Virginia, see Donald Medley et al., "Functional Knowledge of Participants in the Beginning Teacher Assistance Program," *Elementary School Journal*, Vol. 89 (March 1989), pp. 495–510.

8. The idea of "civic incentives" is developed more fully in George Will, *Statecraft as Soulcraft: What Government Does* (New York: Simon and Schuster, 1983).

9. Thanks for the metaphor, of course, are due to Charles Reich, *The Greening of America* (New York: Random House, 1970).

10. For the case of school-level councils in California, see Bruce Fuller and Jo Ann Izu, "Explaining School Cohesion: What Shapes the Organizational Beliefs of Teachers?" *American Journal of Education*, Vol. 94 (August 1986), p. 501–35. Also see Ann Lieberman, ed., *Rethinking School Improvement* (New York: Teacher's College Press, 1986).

11. For a case study of one state's dual pursuit of pedgogical regulation and encouraging more complex instruction, David Cohen, Teaching Practice: Plus ça Change: (East Lansing, Michigan: National Center for Research on Teacher Education, 1988).

12. Robert Slavin, *Cooperative Learning* (New York: Longman, 1983).

13. For example, see Catherine Lewis, "Cooperation and Control in Japanese Nursery Schools," *Comparative Education Review*, Vol. 28, (1984) pp. 69–84.

14. Elizabeth Cohen's work has long focused on how to change the status-order of classrooms, as defined by the children themselves. See Cohen, "Expectation States and Inter-racial Interaction in School Settings," *Annual Review of Sociology*, Vol. 8 (1982), pp. 209–35. Additional examples of how U.S. programs have linked school and community appear in Michael Williams, *Neighborhood Organizing for Urban School Reform* (New York: Teacher's College Press, 1988).

15. Western literature is impoverished on the topic of culture's long-term influence on formal state agencies. Work on social movements is a notable exception. Three papers provide some conceptual leads: Joyce Rothschild-Whitt, "An Alternative to Rational-Bureaucratic Models," *American Sociological Review*, Vol. 44 (August 1979), pp. 509–27; Albert O. Hirschman, *Getting Ahead Collectively: Grassroots Experiences in Latin America* (New York: Pergamon Press, 1984). Ann Swidler, "Culture in Action: Symbols and Strategies," *American Sociological Review*, Vol. 51 (April 1986), pp. 273–86. For a recent and entirely delightful example of culture's (that is, Frank Zappa's) influence on the new state of Czechoslovakia, see "Rock Around the Revolution: Captain Beefheart Meets the President," *The Economist*, February 3, 1990, pp. 95–96.

Index